WHAT PEOPLE ARE SAYING ABOUT ASA

"You guys have inspired me, and I may now double my staff in the next couple of weeks so that we can grow our $7.5M book of business."

—Mark Hanna
Agency Owner

"My state has been experiencing some pretty tough times with rate increases and property concerns. It's been tough. It's also been easy to be disgruntled and consider pulling back to try and save revenue for a better climate. That said, we decided to take a different approach. I joined Agency Sales Academy, and I got my team engaged in coaching and role-playing. We have become more organized in our prospecting efforts. We became determined to sell only on value and coverage. We are trying to make price the least important part of the 'education' process with customers and prospects. We have hired three additional salespeople and ramped up local marketing and COI efforts. This March was the best month my agency has had in 21 years. We issued 350 items. As my newer sales folks learn what you teach at ASA, I believe we will be a 500 to 600 item-per-month agency by June."

—John Rose
Agency Owner

"Thank you for everything ASA has done for us. Since attending the last event, we have reinvented our agency. I've hired a 'closer' for sales and another service agent. We're still on the hunt for more sales staff! I can feel we're on the cusp of great things!"   **—Randall Bogani**
Agency Owner

"The Agency Sales Academy is a great venue for agents to proactively conquer the day-to-day challenges we all face. It has a wealth of information and is incredibly well organized."   **—Jon Allcox**
Agency Owner

"My entire staff are fired up after attending the ASA event. Nothing I have ever done has invigorated my staff and agency manager like your event. So many other programs and presenters are full of hot air. It's invigorating to know that there are others out there like us who are working their very hardest to be the very best. Thank you, ASA!"
—Laure Feld
Agency Owner

"Shout out to Agency Sales Academy! We are at 102 items so far this month, with $60,190 in premium, and eight phone interviews scheduled next week in the search for our next two sales superstars! #ASArocks!"   **—Karen Ross Miller**
Agency Owner

"Outstanding event! A class-act event put on by class-act folks!"
—Maurice Stephens
Agency Owner

"I called back a prospect today who I thought would never close. She had every excuse in the book and couldn't make up her mind about anything. I was nervous that the high monthly premium on her auto insurance would be the deal breaker, but I called her back this afternoon after we got back from the ASA training. I spoke with confidence and an air of professionalism. The price came up only after I reviewed everything. I simply explained, 'We will just set it up on a draft using your routing and account numbers, and the price would be $349 with the multi-policy discount, as we will take care of your renters as well.' It worked! You can bring up the price—even if you think it might be high—once you establish yourself as their trusted partner. We are binding tomorrow."

—Melany Shaw
Agency Support Staff

"Great event! My staff and I got a lot of great points to go work on in our office. Having some of your staff there talking from their respective views was definitely a plus. After 25 years as an agent, I am still learning how to 'build a better mouse trap.'"

—Kirt Lattanze
Agency Owner

"The conference was dynamite! My folks are committed to blowing up their prior sales goals this year. They understand now what is possible and they know that I expect *big time* results from each of them. Thank you!"

—Harley Alloway
Agency Owner

"Going to ASA's event was an incredible experience for myself and the staff member I brought with me. It was time and money well spent. In fact, it was an investment in taking my agency to the next level. I look forward to implementing these great, easy-to-execute ideas."

—Linda Fullman
Agency Owner

INSURANCE
SALES
SECRETS

INSURANCE
SALES
SECRETS

Four Pillars of
Accelerated Agency Growth

JAY ADKINS | KEEFE DUTERTE
GREG GRAY | KEVIN MLYNAREK
DANELLE DELGADO

Contact the authors or publisher if you would like information on how to access any and all programs or other materials associated with this book and its contents.

AgencySalesAcademy.com

This book may be purchased for educational, business, or sales promotional use. For information or to order, please contact:

Agency Sales Academy
128 Killarney Rd
Winfield, West Virginia 25213
1-866-888-4ASA (866-888-4272)
ASA@AgencySalesAcademy.com

ISBN-13: 978-0-578-65347-1

Copyright© 2020 by Agency Sales Academy
First Edition

The Library of Congress Cataloging-in-Publication data on file
Adkins, Delgado, Duterte, Gray, Mlynarek
1st ed. ISBN 978-0-9652201-4-9

Cover and interior designed by Marisa Jackson.

The authors gratefully acknowledge Jennifer Lill Brown for her help in the writing and editing process of this book.

DISCLAIMER

This book is presented solely for educational purposes. The author and publisher are not offering it as legal or financial planning services advice. Every individual and company are different, and the advice and strategies contained herein may not be suitable for your situation.

While best efforts have been used in preparing this book, the authors and publisher make no representations or warranties of any kind and assume no liabilities of any kind with respect to the accuracy or completeness of the contents and specifically disclaim any implied warranties of merchantability or fitness of use for a particular purpose.

Neither the authors nor the publisher shall be held liable or responsible to any person or entity with respect to any loss or incidental or consequential damages caused, or alleged to have been caused, directly or indirectly, by the information or programs contained herein. No warranty may be created or extended by sales representatives or written sales materials.

IdealTraits.com© and AgencyMarketingMachine.com© are companies owned and operated by founders of AgencySalesAcademy.com.

TO OUR LOVING AND DEVOTED FAMILIES

We are forever grateful to you for supporting us and
being there every step of the way as we pursue our
big dreams and work crazy hours. We know we have
sacrificed a lot to achieve what we have.
But none of it would have been possible
or even worth it without you.

We love you!

Table of Contents

REVENUE

OPERATIONS

PREFACE

The One Thing
All Winners Have

Usain Bolt is dubbed The World's Fastest Man. When he was at the height of his record-breaking career, did he really need a coach anymore?

How much faster can you get if you're already the fastest?

Usain Bolt never saw it that way, which is *why* he became known as the fastest man in the world. When asked about the importance of his longtime coach and mentor, Glen Mills, Bolt once said, "He has always made the right decisions for me. He is a guiding light in my career and he has shown me the way to improve myself, both as a person and as an athlete."

In the world of professional sports, the difference between the number one player in the world (someone who everyone recognizes and admires) and being among the top 10 (someone whose name no one even remembers) is often a matter of millimeters or milliseconds.

There is just a tiny splinter of a difference between the very best and all the rest.

It's no different in our careers. There are over a million insurance agents in the United States alone. We're talking about a sea of professionals who all sell the same basic kinds of products and services.

We're *all* the same.

At least that's the way prospective customers see it.

A small part of you might believe that as well. So when you hear success stories about seven- and eight-figure producers, you think, "That guy really got lucky." Or, "She must have been in the right place at the right time."

Success in this business has *nothing* to do with luck. If you dig a little, we predict you will find that every agency success story has one thing in common. It's the single factor that spells the difference between building a legacy and being just another forgettable agent.

Want to know what they all have in common?

They have coaches.

Coaches and mentors give you priceless tools you could never acquire on your own:

1. Vision

A coach provides you with vision. You can't see the label from inside the box, right? Your coach helps you step back and appreciate the big picture, assess the situation, and determine the best move forward. Coaches and mentors can get you on the path to where you want to be because they are already there! The right mentor becomes your lighthouse, a shining beacon to guide you to shore. Without that guide, you are sailing blind.

2. Objectivity

The next gift a coach gives you is objectivity. There is no one more personally invested than you are in your agency, but your attachment to the business can also be a problem. That problem stems from emotion. Emotions cloud decision making, and they can sabotage your business if they are left unchecked. A coach provides you with neutral, objective advice that can get you past dips and roadblocks more effectively. They have not invested the blood, sweat, and tears you have in your agency. This gives them the ability to make decisions without biases and fear getting in the way.

3. Perspective

The next benefit of having a coach is perspective. If you rely only on your personal perspective, you are putting hard limits on the potential of your agency. An outside viewpoint can make all the difference. A mentor's successes and failures can provide perspective that helps you avoid costly mistakes. Just one or two corrections from our coaches have put countless dollars in our pockets over the years and continue to do so.

4. Encouragement

Coaches are your greatest source of encouragement. We are leaders, but that doesn't mean we are immune to the negative attitudes and motivation destroyers that plague everyone else. Your team needs encouragement to stay on target, and so do you. The right coach will challenge you, push you, and inspire you.

As bystanders watching Usain Bolt at the height of his career, it was easy to believe he had reached his limit of sprinting greatness. Again, how much faster can you get than "fastest"? Here is what Bolt's coach had to say about that in an interview:

"I wouldn't say that we have seen the best of him. I think that he's capable of more..."

The coach of the world's fastest man believed he could be faster! He saw untapped potential in a track and field superstar we saw as the preeminent example of greatness and athletic distinction.

Now *that* is both amazing and inspiring.

When you think you've reached your limit, your coach will pull more out of you. When you hit a plateau, your coach will help you find the path to the next level.

You could ask your spouse, best friend, or business partner to be your coach—but typically, you get what you pay for. Ever had a free golf or tennis lesson? We bet you got out of that exactly what you put into it. Nothing.

If you want to be the best, find someone who is already the best, and do what they did. Just understand that you can't expect successful leaders and influencers to give you their insights for free. Their knowledge and experiences are highly valuable.

We pay mentors to help us discover areas that are hurting our agencies, to take our businesses to higher levels, to develop personally, and to foster millionaire mindsets. No matter how much success we continue to have, we will *never* stop paying for mentorship and coaching.

Someone has already done what you're trying to do. Someone else figured it out and can give you the shortcuts you need to avoid some of the failures.

No matter who you are, where you've come from, or what you have achieved, a good mentor is an invaluable asset that everyone needs. The right mentor believes in you even when you don't. Author and motivational speaker Zig Ziglar couldn't have summed it up any better: "A lot of people have gone further than they thought they could because someone *else* thought they could."

Find someone who sees your untapped potential—and let that person or those people help you make smart decisions and think like a millionaire.

We offer coaching programs at Agency Sales Academy that are hand-tailored for this business and designed with agency owners and their staff in mind. Regardless of whether you work with us, we hope you commit to finding a coach who will stand in your corner and show you how to fight for your success.

INTRODUCTION

Success Begins
with Your F.E.E.T.

S ome people are consumed by the trials they face.

Others are built by them.

Massively successful people share a common experience—their greatest triumphs come after their greatest mistakes. How do those rare individuals turn tragedy into triumph? It's actually really simple:

Winners stand back up and keep moving forward.

This means that success is fundamentally about our feet.

Yes, our *feet*.

To this day, you've never gotten anywhere without them. Your feet get you out of bed in the morning. They take you to work every day, and they walk you down the aisle: political aisle, church aisle, grocery store aisle. Your feet quite literally take you everywhere.

They are the unsung heroes of your life.

If you've ever met any of us, you know that we love two things in our businesses almost more than anything else. First, we love to build systems and processes that are based on solid, heartfelt core principles. Second, we love acronyms.

So, we came up with an acronym that represents the values that guide us. Here are the four heartfelt core principles (or the F.E.E.T.) upon which we have built our individual businesses and the Agency Sales Academy:

FUN

We aren't interested in doing dull, monotonous work. We are willing to work hard, but that work better be fun, too! Having fun makes the daily grind feel *less* like a grind and more like a dream career—the kind that gets you excited about getting out of bed in the morning.

EXCELLENCE

Everything we do is centered on excellence, and everyone we choose to work with must also strive for excellence. It's not a buzzword for us—excellence is the *goal* of every interaction and every customer experience. Being excellent differentiates us in a world where everything looks and sounds the same.

EVOLVING

You're either growing or you're dying. We daily resolve to stay humble, teachable, and ready to grow. We'll never believe we have reached the top. The fact that we are alive means there is still plenty of room for improvement.

TRUST

Customers do business with people they like, know, and trust. We want to become Trusted Advisors for our customers, and we also want to leave them better off than they were before they met us. They need to know they can trust us to do everything we promise—and then some. We make it our goal to over-deliver.

Everything we and our team members do and say is based on these four principles. We trust the process. We live it. And we walk it out (with our feet) every day.

We did not say the process is perfect. That's where your feet come in yet again! When something is not working in your business, you can fix it. You stand up, turn around, and walk in a different direction.

Whether you're a brand-new agency owner or an industry veteran, there's always more to learn and new mistakes to be made. But take heart. Real growth comes *through* those mistakes.

Still, it's not a foregone conclusion that you are destined to fail before you accidentally stumble into success. Wouldn't it be great to find a way to transform your business without so many tough lessons?

We think so. In fact, that's why we wrote this book. It contains the four keys to building a thriving, self-sustaining business that produces the best possible outcomes for your customers and your agency.

Making money is important, but we are alive today for purposes far beyond becoming wealthy—and attaining those distinct purposes is what defines *success* to us. When you look at success this way, money simply becomes a means to an end. It buys the time and resources we need to fulfill our real intentions in life.

Still, it's tempting to look at the victories of others and think, "I'll never be as successful as they are. They are just better businesspeople... better at sales... they are smarter... faster... stronger... taller..."

You may have a million reasons why you think you'll never reach *that* level of success. But if you really want to win, the excuses must stop. People who make excuses are just trying to justify their failures, so they don't feel as guilty when they give up.

The better way is to look *behind* others' successes to find the path they took to get there. No doubt you will find it was not a straight road, but a jagged journey of tough lessons and bad choices.

We are all extremely successful. But if you think we just got lucky, had a better territory, or inherited a good book of business, you are mistaken.

We've encountered huge obstacles. We've made horrible decisions. We've hired out of desperation to fill empty seats. We've focused on the bottom line at the expense of employees and customers.

We made massive mistakes and kept going until we figured it out—and luck had nothing to with it.

Allow us to shed some light on our voyage, and yours. We'll begin with a brief history of our individual paths to the present day. Then, it's on to the four pillars of accelerated growth that will give you the foundation for becoming the agency *hero* you've always wanted to be.

JAY'S STORY

The journey toward my multi-state, lucrative insurance business started at Waffle House. Actually, it started *behind the grill* at Waffle House, cooking grits next to a 400-pound cook named Tiny.

Even before the waffles, back in 1991, my life almost took a very different direction. That was the year I received word that I was being deployed to Dhahran, Saudi Arabia, to defend our country as an air-man in the United States Air Force. They told me I had 48 hours to pack a bag and get on a plane. At that moment, I realized somebody else would have complete control of my life once I got on that plane—and I had learned at a young age that I did not like being controlled.

I made the critical decision to leave the military and instead become a state highway patrol officer. I saw it as a job that would provide me with some of the same structure I had enjoyed in the Air Force without as much of the control, and I was excited about this new direction.

While studying to become a patrolman, a friend of mine who was a manager at a local Waffle House asked me for a favor. "Hey, I've got to recruit people as part of my job. Could you just come in for an interview?"

I shook my head. "Listen man, I will *never* work at Waffle House."

He persisted, and I agreed to come in just to help boost his recruiting numbers.

I interviewed with the manager of a local Waffle House, and within seconds, I *knew* it wasn't for me. I cut the meeting short and began to walk out of the building. However, two Waffle House executives stopped me before I reached my car and asked me to stay for a few more minutes.

Fast-forward 48 hours—and there I stood beside a cook named Tiny, watching him scatter, cover, and smother some hash browns and fry some eggs.

Fast-forward another four and a half years—and I had become a regional manager for Waffle House, handling $35 million of business a year. It wasn't because I was the smartest or the most qualified. Waffle House had systems in place, and thanks to my Air Force background, processes and systems had become a vital part of my daily life. I followed every process to a tee and worked the systems with military precision.

Soon after, New York Life, our country's largest mutual life insurance company, recruited me to work for them. It was a great opportunity at first, but it quickly became a struggle because I felt like I was always going through the *back door*.

Prospects would ask, "Do you offer home and auto insurance?"

Inevitably, I'd have to say, "No, but I know someone who does."

After about the hundredth time of hearing that question and passing good leads to other agents who had the products those prospects really wanted, I knew something had to change. I wanted to go through the *front door* and stop passing business off to other people. I realized I was growing other agents' bottom lines with business that was sitting directly in front of me.

Soon after, I was recruited into a management position at Allstate, a role I worked diligently in for over a year.

Then one day, an opportunity knocked me in the face. A top-performing Allstate agent asked me, "So, Jay, what do you like about management?"

"It's a pretty good gig. I make good money and get to work with great agents."

The agent pulled out a check and asked, "Do you make this much?"

I nodded, "Oh yeah, I definitely make more than that in a year."

The agent paused before clarifying, "Jay, this is what I make in a *month*."

That was all I needed to hear. I became an agent, and then I started my own agency from scratch in 2001. I made plenty of mistakes in the beginning—too many to list. But after a few years, I realized that there were people out there who already knew all the answers to the questions I had.

After I started leaning on the guidance of incredible mentors, my agency exploded.

I found the success I always wanted.

I then started looking into acquisitions, but I was told by numerous colleagues that I'd *never* be able to have agencies in multiple states.

Those who know me know that I will do whatever it takes to prove naysayers and cynics wrong—and I also don't like to lose. Today, I have hugely successful agencies in Texas, North Carolina, and Florida.

From grilling waffles to creating a multi-state insurance business, I finally found my calling. I always say that as an agent, you are the second most important professional in people's lives, right behind their doctor. Agents both *protect* people's assets and help *build* people's assets. And that's a reason to get up in the morning.

DANELLE'S STORY

My path to the present makes no sense on paper. If you had told me as a little girl that I'd go to nursing school and then become a teacher, landscaper, youth minister, mom, top sales performer, online business entrepreneur, and success coach for some of the biggest thought leaders in the world, I'd think you were crazy or hilarious. Or maybe both.

In the beginning, I was confident about my path. I was *sure* I wanted to be a nurse, and so that's what I pursued. I excelled in my nursing classes, but honestly, I hated it. I ended up quitting one year before finishing my studies.

The next logical step, in my mind anyway, was teaching. Always the overachiever, I attended the University of Northern Colorado and double majored in middle school education and earth sciences. I enjoyed the idea of being a teacher, but once I was actually teaching, I became bored. Like, really bored.

I started to understand the concept of creating multiple streams of income, so I opened up a lawn company on the side. I enjoyed the work and the distraction it gave me from my day job, but I knew it wasn't my purpose. I wanted to make a difference. I felt like I could have a bigger impact.

My path soon led me into youth work—and when I do things, I do them big. I took a struggling youth group from ten kids to 250 kids within the first two years. We grew, and our impact grew right along with us. I eventually had three full-time staff members and 20 interns.

I loved the work, but it wasn't generating enough income. So, I added two more jobs to the mix. I started writing marketing materials for a large company and speaking at youth and women's events. I was gone from home a lot, and the hours and travel were hard on me, my small children, and my marriage.

My marriage soon fell apart. There I was, alone with three kids—a three-year-old and two-year-old twins. It was now up to me to provide the life for them that I always dreamed they'd have. What was I going to do?

I knew I had to find a way to earn more. I also knew I didn't want to pursue the "work two jobs and put my kids in daycare" route. I decided I had to create a home-based business.

I was introduced to sales by some extremely wealthy top earners (high six figures a month) in a prominent multi-level marketing company. These titans taught me the art of sales, and I eventually rose in the ranks to become a top earner myself. I was even featured as a guest judge on NBC's The Apprentice because of my success.

I had become my own boss and was amply providing for my kids. Still, something didn't feel right. Money is important, but I soon learned it isn't everything. I felt a disconnect with selling things that didn't greatly impact change.

I was winning, but I wasn't helping others win. I kept hearing a voice telling me that my true calling was to help other people monetize their own gifts.

In the midst of this existential crisis, a real crisis manifested. I had been having crazy hot flashes, mood swings, and other symptoms that typically only happen at a much older age. I knew something was really wrong. My gut told me to see a specialist.

The diagnosis was thyroid cancer.

I immediately felt the fleeting nature of my existence, and I decided, while battling the cancer, that I'd also fight for the life I really wanted. A life that would leave a legacy, not just a large inheritance for my kids.

I created my own company called Life Intended, a company whose moral compass I'd be able to direct and control. I developed relationships with the world's top trainers, coaches, and influencers.

I built a thriving international business while working from home, recovering from cancer, and raising three small children.

I crossed paths with the guys at Agency Sales Academy a few years ago. There was an instant alignment of our hearts and minds, and I knew I wanted to build a business with them.

I saw the life I wanted, and I let nothing stand in my way. Things are never going to be perfect. And if you wait for the stars to align before you start pursuing your true purpose, you'll always live with regret. Put it all on the table and create the life you want now! The only one stopping you is *you*.

KEEFE'S STORY

When I bought my first insurance agency at 27 years old, I thought I had it all figured out. In my mind, my first business plan might as well have been printed on gold paper. *It was magical. It was pure perfection.* That is, until it wasn't. Like the great philosopher Mike Tyson once said, "Everybody has a plan until they get punched in the mouth."

I got punched in the mouth for three long years. From 2007 to 2010, my numbers went in the wrong direction. I effectively took a *mega* agency and turned it into a *large* agency. I lost $1,346,230 in premium alone. I also hired *and* fired 26 people during that time.

Not exactly the outcome I had envisioned.

Something had to change. I had to make a decision—and that decision involved asking for help. I never sought help before because I felt it made me look weak. But what I discovered is that we don't ask for help because we're weak…

We ask for help so that we can stay strong!

After I started seeking the counsel of mentors in this business, things started to turn around quickly. I began to see real money come into my agency, and my burning question then became, "What can I do to make even more money?"

I began expanding my business, booking talks, and flying across the country.

Who paid the price for this success? My family. One day, as I was packing for another trip, my daughter came into the room. "Dad, you are leaving *again*?"

"Yes, honey, I gotta go hop on a plane."

My daughter sighed. "Can't you figure out how to work from home, just for today?"

I picked her up and put her on the bed. "Honey, this is how I make money for our family. This is how I put a roof over your head and food on the table; how you get to go to horse lessons and soccer practice."

She looked up at me with big, sad eyes. "I don't care about that stuff. I just want you."

That pivotal conversation prompted some important questions: When will enough be enough? What amounts of money, success, awards, and recognition would make me feel fulfilled? What does "enough" even look like? When will I give myself permission to make my family my top priority?

The people we care about spell "love" with the letters T-I-M-E—and I realized I was giving them none of it because I had screwed up my own definition of success.

Zig Ziglar once said, "I believe that being successful means having a balance of success stories across the many areas of your life. You can't truly be considered successful in your business life if your home life is a shambles."

I could relate to that. Finally, after discovering and implementing the four pillars explained in this book, I had achieved even *more* success in my agencies, and most importantly, my family had their dad and husband back.

GREG'S STORY

A lot of people seem to have it all figured out when they're young. They know what they want to be, or least they have an idea of what really inspires then.

I wasn't one of those people.

During the second semester of my junior year in college, I was asked to come to the career counselor's office. After I inquired as to the whereabouts of this alleged counseling office, I found my way to him and heard *the* question.

"You're almost a senior, Greg. You have to declare a major. What's it going to be?"

My response: "What do I have the most hours in so far?"

"Communications."

"Well, then. It looks like communications is the winner."

After college, I did what anyone with a degree in communications would do. I became a furniture salesman. Predictably, I quickly grew tired of the grind and monotony of this position. There was no real room for growth, and it was decidedly uninspiring.

I did what I never thought I'd do, which was to go work for my father, who was a district manager for Zales. I went from selling furniture to selling jewelry. It still wasn't particularly inspiring, but my father instilled in me the mentality that *expecting to win* is the only way to operate in life. His mental fortitude and overall attitude toward his work and his customers became etched within me and shaped the type of professional, leader, and trainer I would one day become.

After I left Zales, I went to work for MCI, a long-distance phone company. I enjoyed the sales process, but what I really enjoyed was helping others do their job well. I loved watching that aha moment appear on people's faces when they realize, "I finally get it!" Unfortunately, I never seemed to be organized enough to compete for any of the corporate trainer positions that came my way.

As fate would have it, our company sent a few of us to a business development seminar. As I sat in a Holiday Inn conference room in Augusta, Georgia, with 60 other people, I was enthralled by what the trainer was saying.

Then I had my own aha moment. This corporate trainer, Bob Summers, was getting $200 a ticket for each us. Sure, he was out of pocket for some light snacks and the fee to rent this little room for two days—but then he was free to keep what was left of that $12,000.

This was it! I knew I wanted to be an entrepreneur and figure out to how impact change through a one-to-many training model. I went back to my day job but was officially on the hunt for the right opportunity to present itself.

I ran into that same trainer a short time later and got my chance. Bob and I struck up a conversation, and he filled me in on an opportunity. His was one of four bids remaining in the running for a huge contract with the U.S. Postal Service. Should his bid win the contract, he'd need fellow trainers to help him implement a training program nationwide to 150,000 USPS employees over nine months.

I went home and typed up my letter of resignation to MCI, even though the contract hadn't yet been won. I didn't print it out or turn in my letter. I just kept it there on my word processor (old school computer) and simply changed the date every morning.

A few months later, the call came in. We got the contract! I printed and signed my resignation letter and delivered it to my boss. I was ready to forge my new path to training.

I traveled to 500 different cities during our time with USPS. After the contract ended, new doors opened for me, and I found myself working as a contract trainer for the esteemed Franklin Covey group.

While working for Franklin Covey, I was invited by Allstate to do some training for them. That was 1999. All these years later, I've continued working with Allstate as a trainer in the areas of customer service, leadership, and sales. My specialty is helping people and organizations turn problems into opportunities.

In my dealings with Allstate, I ran into a guy named Jay Adkins who was always at the top of the company. He'd forgotten the charger for his MacBook, and I was one of the only people at the time (besides him) who had one. I shared my cord, and we became fast friends.

A few years later, he approached me. "I have an opportunity for you," Jay began.

"I don't even need to know what it is. I'm in."

I didn't need to know, because Jay is the kind of person anyone would want to have as a business partner. He's just a winner. A few months later, I was on stage with the rest of the ASA team.

My winding, meandering road to the present day is proof that your true path will chase you. You can run from it. You can try to hide. You can evade it for years. But once you embrace it, it's like the windows of heaven open. Today, I am truly blessed to be able to provide people with a shortcut back to their own paths—and onto the road to where they really want to be.

KEVIN'S STORY

There was a time in my life when I felt like I was stuck on the sidelines. In high school, I was the best golfer on my team, and I was among the best of the best golfers in our district. My successes in high school were enough to earn a golf scholarship to Eastern Michigan University, which got me on the team—but not in the action. It turns out I wasn't good enough to play at that level. I became an alternate, and I was stuck practicing for tournaments in which I'd never participate.

After a year or so of watching other people play, I decided it was time to let that dream go and start pursuing some new ones. I began working two, sometimes three jobs at a time—anything to make enough money to save for my big future and avoid going deeper into debt from college tuition and expenses.

After graduation, my original plan was to go to law school the next fall. However, making more money became a priority to help pay for the huge expense of law school. I started working at a law firm for $9.00 an hour. That wasn't going to cut it. Because of my lifelong interest in cars, I decided that working at a car dealership could be a good fit (and the new car that came with the position sounded like a great perk).

I interviewed at a Dodge dealership, but after four rounds of interviewing and no offer, I moved on to another dealership group. One personality profile test and two intimidating interviews later, the new car sales manager said, "Based on the results of your test, you have what we are looking for. We'd like you to start Monday."

The new job was a far cry from a law career, but I loved it. I was making money instead of spending it, but most importantly, I was surrounded by some incredible business minds that would help create the value-based selling foundation and learning environment I needed to succeed.

After outperforming my peers and following my dad's recommendation to "dress for the job you want, not the job you have," I was promoted to sales manager. At just 22 years old, I was managing salespeople twice my age who had been in the business for years! It was a challenging experience to say the least.

While I was working at the dealership one day, a beautiful young woman walked in looking to sell the dealership some advertising. What she ended up with was a husband.

My wife Jen and I began to grow our family, but my long hours at the dealership were tremendously hard on everyone, especially my kids. I worked from 7 A.M. until 10 P.M. When I left in the morning, my kids were asleep. When I got home at night, my kids were asleep.

Something had to change. I realized that becoming an entrepreneur and being my own boss might be the answer. Still, I was nervous about the large initial investment and complete uncertainty of when the next paycheck would come, where it would come from, and how much it would be. I finally decided to fight past the fear and find a way to carve out more time with my family.

I spent a year carefully researching what I wanted to do before I opened my first insurance agency in 2007. The learning curve from car sales to insurance sales was a steep one. There were so many things to learn, and quite frankly, I didn't know what I didn't know!

After struggling with many unknowns, I realized I had to surround myself with the best business minds, those who had "been there, done that" and were still doing it.

Five years later, after becoming a student of the business, making painful and expensive mistakes, and learning from the best, I was named Allstate's "Best in Company" two years in a row in 2012 and 2013.

I was working for myself, spending more time with my family, and making more money than ever. No more late nights! Jen, our children Gabriel, Macy, and Marissa, and I now experience more joy as a family than I could have ever imagined all those years ago, when I was standing on the sidelines, wishing I were in the action.

GET READY TO BE A H.E.R.O.

We are living proof you don't have to work more to make more.

It *is* possible to design a business that balances work with life. You don't have to choose one over the other! It's about building a business so good and so fundamentally strong that it produces the same results whether you're at the office or on an extended vacation with your family.

It's time to overcome your misconceptions about success. It's also time to dispel the myth that you have to transform your whole business or work more hours in order to maximize revenue. That's simply not true; in fact, *small* changes are often the key.

Big improvements come from small shifts in thinking, or even from the implementation of a single new process. It's not about the big stuff. We believe, as businessman and inspirational author W. Clement Stone once said, "Big doors swing on little hinges."

In this book, you will discover how to make incremental changes to your agency that lead to accelerated growth. You can transform your business by taking one step at a time and by employing one of the most powerful tools you have: Focus.

Steve Jobs perfectly summarized focus like this:

"People think focus means saying *yes* to the thing you've got to focus on. But that's not what it means at all. It means saying *no* to the hundred other good ideas that there are. You have to pick carefully. I'm actually as proud of the things we haven't done as the things I have done. Innovation is saying no to 1,000 things."

We know you've been to trainings. You've read books. You've been told a lot of things. There's a lot of noise out here, and it's easy to start thinking, "How do I do it all?"

You don't! We've narrowed down all the noise into four distinct areas of focus, and those form the basis of our H.E.R.O. system:

HIRING

ENVIRONMENT

REVENUE

OPERATIONS

These are the four pillars that will make the greatest impact on your business. If you can become really skilled at *hiring*, focus on building an agency *environment* that fosters learning and accelerated growth, and put systems and processes into place that automate *operations*, the end result will be reduced costs and increased *revenue*.

You have chosen a career in insurance. Now it's time to use your feet (and F.E.E.T.) to walk in the right direction. But don't do it alone—there is no need to be a lone wolf when there are plenty of people and resources out there that can help you accelerate your growth. For more information on our coaching programs that are designed to help you focus on the four pillars of agency excellence, visit:

AgencySalesAcademy.com/coaching

H

HIRING

If You Only
Read One Chapter

Y ou've got a lot going on in your head right now. You're wondering, among other things, if reading this book is going to be worth
your time. It could be you've already told yourself this is "just another
business book" and you'll read a few chapters before you get distracted
by something else.

We get it. We're busy, too.

We also know that not every book is absorbed cover to cover by its
readers. And while we believe that your business will grow beyond even
your most ambitious expectations by learning about all four parts of the
H.E.R.O. system, we need you to know one huge, undeniable truth:

**If your agency isn't a living, breathing, endlessly developing
training machine, the rest of this book won't do you much good.**

Let's say that after you read this book, you implement a concierge
program like the ones we have in our agencies. Great! If your salespeople

and staff aren't properly trained on how to show customers all the benefits of such programs, you will have just wasted your time and energy.

Or, let's say you decide to use our ten-step hiring process that is designed to attract sales superstars. Awesome! If you don't make ongoing training a part of your agency culture after you bring on those superstars, you'll continually bleed employees and eventually revert back to your current hiring practice (we're guessing it's the "hire a warm body" approach).

Without the right training, you are setting yourself and your agency up for huge disappointment, frustration, and mediocrity.

Most agencies are mediocre. If you want to be average, that's your choice. Stop reading and just keep doing what you're doing, and all your dreams of mediocrity will come true!

If that doesn't sound good, then read this chapter. You may not finish the book. We hope you do, but if you read only one chapter, it has to be this one.

WHAT TRAINING ISN'T

Before we dive in, we need to dispel a few training myths. To a lot of people, the word "training" means attending a five-day course or watching online sales tutorials.

This flawed definition of training, more than anything else—more than the number of calls your agents are making, more than the competition, more than the economy, more than stiffened regulations, more than a saturated market—is the reason agencies fail.

Training is not an event. It is not a static series of tutorials. It is not a seminar.

All of those things can be a part of training. But *real* training, the kind that brings massive success to everyone on your team, begins at the first interview, where you set the expectation that your agency is a living, breathing, evolving training machine.

Then, it continues every day, right up until the moment you decide you've made enough money.

In this chapter, we are going to cover the who, what, when, where, how, and why of training. We are going to teach you what to do, how to do it, and then explain *why* we do it that way.

You can't miss this if you're ready to start experiencing explosive agency growth.

THE REAL WINNERS IN THE TRAINING GAME

In businesses that revolve around a culture of training, there are no losers. With the right training and coaching, everyone in an agency, and everyone who deals with that agency, will win.

Obviously, your staff benefits from training—and not just new hires. Every employee, no matter the position and no matter how long the tenure, should be included in the training process.

We train our new salespeople. We train our seasoned salespeople. We train our retention specialists. We train our managers. We train our customer service team. The training may look a little different, but it happens at every level.

When you hire new agents, they need a lot of shaping. What is the major insurance companies' solution for that? A three-day or five-day training course.

Think about the absurdity of that for a minute by considering this: If you want to make the most money in a career outside of sales, what do you need? You'll need the right degree and the right experience. If you want to be a doctor, that means a lot of school and a lot of hands-on training in a hospital before you are ever allowed to treat your own patients. If you want to be a top business executive in a prominent organization, you need an MBA, and you definitely need a lot of relevant real-world experience.

Big salaries equate to big learning. There is no such thing as easy money. The "experts" of the world are the ones who earn top dollar.

Three days of training during your first week on the job—even two weeks or two months of training—isn't going to cut it. Would you trust a car mechanic who has only been working on cars for a month to repair your new car? Would you trust a lawyer to represent you in court who has only had her law degree for a week? Would you trust a doctor to perform surgery on you without years of the proper training?

Are we really equating what we do to the work of doctors and lawyers?

Absolutely we are.

You'll hear us say this over and over again: As your customers' insurance agent, you are the second most important professional in their lives. Their doctor is first because he or she keeps them alive. You are second—because you protect everything in that life they love, value, and need.

What you do is critical. Don't ever forget that. It may not be glamorous but make no mistake: You offer something that everyone you will ever come into contact with needs. Besides doctors and medical professionals, no other vocation can make that claim.

In order to become Trusted Advisors (more on that term in a few chapters) in the eyes of your customers, your staff must become educated in every part of the business—product knowledge, industry expertise, relationship building, effective follow-up, efficient business practices, the use of technology and social media, phone skills, people skills, how to find needs, how to close, how to network, how to ask for referrals, how to build retention, and more.

That impressive list of skills isn't learned in three days or even three years.

Instilling a culture of training in your agency positions your staff and your customers to win. Prioritizing training above all else also cuts the learning curve for new people and helps them make money faster, which lessens frustration and prevents turnover.

In our business, 94 percent of agents say they are not getting any development beyond the first week or two in their new positions.

That is unacceptable.

It's been years since we've lost an agent we didn't want to lose—and that is because of our rigorous hiring process that is followed by our continual training process.

As an agency owner, you also win big with the right training. Every time you see your staff learn a new element of the business or break past a plateau, your commitment to ongoing training will be reinforced. Your revenue will increase, and you'll avoid the tremendous frustration that comes from having high turnover.

Set the tone from the first interview that you are running a training-based organization. Let them know you will set clear expectations every step of the way. Then reassure them that you won't just throw them into the deep end. You'll guide them into the water, teach them how to swim, and explain why the movements you are teaching keep them afloat.

After we hire, we always keep our word. Within the first few weeks, if they haven't met the well-defined expectations and benchmarks we set, they're out. No exceptions. We'd rather lose them in the beginning than have them quit after months of wasted time and opportunities.

If a discussion about training and accountability scares candidates away, that is fine with us. Our hiring process is more about weeding out the bad than it is about hiring the good. In fact, we consistently "run off" about 90 percent of the people we interview.

The end result is an agency full of winners who are coachable and hungry for success.

THE MOST EFFECTIVE TRAINING SYSTEM

Right now, there is a good chance you're thinking, "This sounds like a lot of work."

It is—but not as much as you think. In the beginning, as you develop your standards and practices for training, it will be time intensive. You'll need to create a training timeline, daily coaching agendas, and training standards and practices. After you develop your training process and put it in motion, there will initially be kinks, but after a while, your training machine will become its own autonomous life force in the office that is a valuable part of everyone's daily routine.

If you want to reach this level of training automation, you'll need a system in place and a method to your madness. In our agencies, we follow the "Five M's of Training," as taught by legendary business and success mentor John Maxwell:

Step 1: Model

The first thing you ask your staff to do when they are learning something new is to observe. They listen and observe you, a manager, or another staff member undertaking a task such as using a piece of technology, calling on a new lead, closing business, or following up with a customer on the phone. Show them how it looks when it's done correctly. This provides them with a benchmark and a model to follow.

Step 2: Mentor

After employees watch you perform a task at least two times, they must assist in the process and explain to you why everyone in your agency does it this way. The old "show and do" model of training is ineffective because it skips this step. It doesn't give employees the chance to understand the why. Asking staff members to blindly mimic your actions will never lead to accelerated growth. This step allows them to internalize the action because they get to see and then explain why it's important. Have them describe each step so they *internalize* rather than attempt to memorize.

Step 3: Monitor

In step three, you do the more traditional coaching jobs of assisting and correcting. What's most important in this stage is to be encouraging and patient. Move on only once they can explain it all and do the task successfully.

One of the best ways to monitor your staff is to record their phone calls with customers. We record every conversation that takes place through our agencies' phone systems. Each week, we listen to our team's phone calls, and we use those recordings to reinforce key teaching points. Doing this serves two important purposes: 1) It keeps employees focused all day, because they have no idea which conversation you'll hear, and 2) It gives you valuable material to utilize in future training sessions.

It's easy to set up a recording function on most phone systems. Do it today—you'll be glad you did. Be sure to tell employees that their phone calls will be recorded, and you'll be listening to some of those phone calls with them each week to uncover opportunities for improvement.

Step 4: Motivate

This step is more complicated than it sounds; the reason is that many of us leader-types struggle with patience. It is certainly a virtue—and it's an elusive one. To be a good motivator, you have to be patient. Not everyone is going to learn at a swift pace. It just won't happen. You have to strike that balance between motivating them from the sidelines with stepping in from time to time to correct.

Don't correct enough, and they internalize wrong practices.

Step in too often, and they lose all confidence.

Great coaches let you know when you are doing something right before they ever highlight an area that needs improvement. If you are listening in on a call, and an agent completely skips rapport building and goes right to a quote, you can't just lean over and whisper, "Psst, you missed a step."

People don't respond well to that kind of correction. Instead, celebrate their successes, and then listen to the recorded call together. More often than not, they will notice their missteps and point them out without you having to bring them up at all (the best agents are usually self-critical). You praise them for being so observant, revisit the areas where improvement is needed, and move forward.

Over time and through consistent training, you'll learn everyone's coaching preferences. Some people like the "rah, rah" type of motivation and some don't. The more you get to know your team, the easier this becomes.

Step 5: Multiply

The final step is a miracle maker. When you *really* want to teach someone to do something, have them teach someone else how to do it. The best way to learn something is to teach it. We have agents who've been with us for only a few weeks show newer agents how something is done. It's amazing to watch. You can actually *see* how empowered they feel as they explain a procedure to a less experienced agent.

No matter how long an employee has been with you, that person has something to teach. Let your staff impress you with their knowledge and become even better by sharing that knowledge with others. This is how the best business practices will multiply exponentially within your agency and enable you to duplicate success over and over again.

FINDING THE TIME TO TRAIN

"How do I find the time to train my team?"

It's the age-old question that plagues our industry. In the first few years of our agencies, to say our pace was "frantic" is putting it nicely. We were making calls, interviewing, and trying to grow our business any way we could. On paper, we definitely didn't have time to train. So, what did we do?

The short answer is we made the time to train.

The shorter answer is we prioritized.

Everyone has the same 24 hours available to them in a day. Warren Buffett, Jeff Bezos, and Bill Gates have 24 hours, too. Somehow, they've managed to find the time for making money.

In our business, effective training is the most direct route to making more money. Therefore, it deserves high-priority status. The first things on your calendar every day should represent what matters most—and that is why we train first thing in the morning, every morning.

If it's not on your calendar, then honestly, it doesn't mean all that much to you.

If money isn't your thing, then don't schedule daily training. However, if you want a successful agency, training and role-playing need to be the first things you and your agents do together in the morning.

WHEN

Actions express priorities.

Make training a priority. If you don't, it will never get done. Once the office opens and the phones start ringing, training will get pushed to the back burner every time.

If you don't have enough time in the morning, then rethink your morning. Wake up earlier, come into the office earlier, or open your doors 30 minutes later. Do something, anything, and everything you can to prioritize training above all else.

For individual training sessions with new agents and existing employees, put something on the calendar a few times a month with each team member, if not every week. This is the time when you go over their phone calls and discover opportunities to get better.

During one-on-one sessions, we use a "coaching score card." The card includes a checklist of skills and actions that help agents do their jobs successfully. When we walk through the card with them, something amazing happens. Most agents immediately point out the areas where they could improve.

For new agents, score card meetings may last up to two hours. For others, the meeting is usually less than an hour. Yes, that is a significant time commitment, but you can't afford *not* to do it. If you are not training your staff, they'll either quit or stay and consistently underperform, which means you'll eventually have to let them go.

When do you train your employees?

Only on the days you want to win.

THE BEST PLACES TO TRAIN

WHERE

Team trainings should take place in a conference room to limit distractions. At their desks, the temptation to check email or look at their phone may become too great. One-on-one training can happen at a desk, but ideally you should go to a designated training desk or the manager's office where there will be fewer distractions.

Our conference room trainings are lively sessions where everyone is encouraged to participate, and one person never does all the talking. We stick to a pre-set agenda so that the team knows exactly what they will be learning that day. They can come prepared with questions and ready to role-play with their colleagues.

Role-playing happens daily in our agencies. An agent can nod his head and say, "I understand" all day long, but until you see him do it, you never really know. In fact, if an agent says he gets it but is unwilling or hesitant to demonstrate the skill, then he definitely does not "get it."

The beauty of doing group training and role-playing is that every agent ends up teaching during the meeting, and the agents observing the role-play can learn just as much as those who are participating.

We tell our staff and remind ourselves to never let *ego* get in the way of training. If someone has a better way to do something, then great! Let them demonstrate it, learn from it, and everyone will be better for it.

MAKING IT HAPPEN, EVERY SINGLE DAY

Right now, you probably either overthink training or you don't think about it enough.

Some agency owners believe they need a foolproof system or formal, expensive training. What ends up happening? Nothing. Expensive training programs are rarely, if ever, worth their price tags.

Other agency owners make nothing but desperation hires and follow no real training plan at all. They wake up one day and realize their idea of training is sticking a new agent on the phone and

HOW

feeling frustrated when she quits a short time later. They throw agents to the wolves, and yet they are somehow surprised when the agents get devoured.

No one is born knowing how to do a job skillfully. If you wanted to teach a child how to read or do algebra, it wouldn't do any good for you to say, "Just go do it."

It's the same for your team! In fact, if it helps, think of your employees as your "kids." Don't throw them into the ocean with no life vest. Give them the skills they need to swim.

After you have made training a daily priority, come up with a simple plan for training. It doesn't have to be elaborate. It just needs to be done consistently. Here's an example:

- *Monday:* How to ask for referrals
- *Tuesday:* How to establish rapport over the phone
- *Wednesday:* How to get past the most common stalls and close over the phone
- *Thursday:* How to increase retention using social media, mail, and email
- *Friday:* How to add an umbrella policy to every household

Decide on a topic for every day that month and stick to the plan.

After a while, the group training will run itself. And unlike most meetings—where one person delivers a monologue while everyone else tries not to fall asleep—your people will be getting so much valuable insight that they'll wish the training would continue.

Your team *can* get excited about meetings. It happens all the time in our agencies.

Here are a few more training basics:

1. Have Patience

The only way to be successful is to be patient—in fact, that is your number one job as a coach and a trainer. The rule of thumb is to have *patience* when it's a teaching moment, and to *push* when it's a motivation issue.

It's your agents' job to be coachable. Training will never work if they aren't. If you are teaching someone, and they respond with a comment like, "Well, that's not the way we did it at my old agency," then you have more than likely hired the wrong person.

Do your best to determine whether a person is coachable *before* you make the hire. We tell our agents, "Don't feed your ego; feed your bank account. It's not about what you already know. It's about what you don't know, and it's also about what you didn't even *know* you don't know."

It's their job to remain teachable, and it's yours to be prepared and patient. Don't expect them to do their job if you can't do yours.

2. Don't Ask the Stupid Question

There is one question during any training situation that we recommend you avoid:

"Do you understand?"

How will employees naturally respond to that? They will *never* say no, because that would make them feel stupid. Another awful question to ask is, "Does that make sense?"

When you show them how to do something, don't ask your staff if they understand. Instead, just say, "Now explain it to me."

After they explain it, you say, "Okay, now show me."

3. Reverse Engineer

Use reverse engineering in your training. You accomplish this by starting from the end and helping them figure out how to get there. What steps must be taken to get to the desired result? If they are able to lay it all out successfully, then they can be the ones to identify where they are taking missteps rather than you always having to point it out to them.

4. Practice!

One truth about this career is universal. We hear no—a lot. There is no shortage of disappointment in a sales job. That is the life we've chosen. Luckily, the money and freedom make up for the rejection. One of the best ways for your agents to learn how to take some of the emotion out of hearing no is to practice over and over again. Practice is the *only* tool we have to build confidence in this profession.

THE REAL MOTIVATION BEHIND IT ALL

WHY

If you're not growing, you're dying. This idea needs to be engrained into your consciousness. Make it your daily goal to stay humble and learn, because there is no way you could ever know it all. *Learn something new every day.*

What we are all striving for is growth. Without it, we become stagnate. Sadly, the reason most agencies *believe* they fail is because of tired excuses like, "The market is too saturated" and "It's so hard to find good people."

It's really not that hard. It just takes longer, and requires a hiring system and a training system. Most agency owners are too lazy to put those into place—so they make quick-fix hires, throw hapless agents into the deep end, and become indignant when agents aren't ultra-successful.

If you want to mold raw talent into refined, sharp-selling top agents, it takes time and training. There are no silver bullets or "life hacks" for this step of the process. Unfortunately, we live in a "life hack" culture. We've come to believe there is a quick fix for everything.

What can you get now? Forget tomorrow! Forget ten years from now!

People are not willing to wait, and the truth that some things don't add value immediately is a tough one to grasp for many agency owners.

Training and coaching are investments that pay off—eventually. Sometimes, you see the fruits of your labor right away. When a new agent rocks a call after training, you are instantly filled with pride and the agent gets a jolt of confidence. But then he can't get any traction for the rest of that day and goes home totally deflated.

Scenarios like that happen daily in this business.

Are you willing to keep training? Do you understand that the time you take with your agents is what will determine how high your agency will go?

Don't expect your employees to get it after a single training session or even a dozen sessions. Your goal is not for them to get 100 percent better or have some magical aha moment.

You just want them to grow by 1 percent. That's all.

If they grow just 1 percent better each time they train, and they train every day, five days a week, 25 times a month—you can do the math. Over time, they are going to grow 100, 200, and 300 times better. Eventually, their growth will be exponential.

Everybody wants to come to work and feel like they are growing. We are not just talking about the new, inexperienced people. Star players are going to be star players somewhere, and if you don't give them the opportunity to sharpen their skills in your agency, they are going to find a place where they can.

Smart agency owners have a well-defined growth path for their team members. We know the top performing agents are not going to be content to earn mediocre commissions year after year.

They want to see the potential for more. Paint the picture for them in the interview. Tell them that top agents become managers, and managers who excel can run their own agency one day. One of greatest joys you'll ever experience is to see people spread their wings and fly after you have given them every opportunity to succeed.

Can you imagine a basketball or soccer coach sending players out onto the court or field with no direction? That coach wouldn't have a job for long.

Your players want training. Do your job. Give them what they want and need.

In our agencies, we write between 500 and 600 policies a month. Average agencies write 45.

Want to get to our level? It's not rocket science. It's not even talent, intelligence, or business acumen.

It's training.

Fix the
Broken Process

In 1983, Gary Keller and Joe Williams opened a small real estate office in Austin, Texas. After just two years in business, Keller Williams became the largest single-office residential real estate firm in Austin.

Today, they are the largest real estate franchise in the United States. Do you know how many team members they started with in 1983? According to Gary Keller, they had just six agents. They grew from half a dozen agents to 72 agents in just two years.

How did they do it?

They hired the right people, who hired the right people, who hired the right people...

Real estate is seen as a "low barrier to entry" kind of industry (much like insurance). However, not all real estate agencies will hire anyone with a license. When you interview with Keller Williams, expect to go back a second time if the first face-to-face interview goes well. Then a third.

Keller Williams CEO Mark Willis explains why. He says the first interview is entirely scripted and includes a personality and behavioral profile. If you don't raise any red flags during stage one, you'll be called back for a second, more comprehensive interview. If you get called back a third time, be prepared to express the depth of your commitment to Keller Williams, and much more.

Why go through such lengths to vet someone who may or may not be around in a few months?

With such high turnover in most sales positions, is all that effort even worth it?

These are two questions that resonate with those of us in the insurance field. Unfortunately, it is also exactly that type of questioning that has led our sector to use the subpar recruiting practices that have led to industry-wide mediocrity and frustration.

Before we can talk about how to fix the broken hiring system, let's discuss how we got into this mess in the first place.

CHURN AND BURN

For years, the model for hiring in our industry has been the "warm body" approach. It is a hiring method that was born out of necessity.

An agency sales position is one of the toughest jobs on the planet, and it's not for everyone. As agency owners, we know that the rewards far outweigh the difficulties. However, we also know that plenty of people are not cut out for the extreme highs and lows of a career in sales.

Are you resilient? Are you willing to push past failure? Do you see the value of relationship building in business? Are you able to brush off a refusal as just a refusal, and not take it as an indictment of you as a human being? Can you be empathetic to customer concerns, no matter how insignificant they may seem to you?

These are qualities that only a select few possess.

Given the difficulties that come with the position and the rare mix of abilities required to do the job well, it's easy to see why the churn-and-burn trend started. But why are we still adhering to this philosophy when it's not working, and never really has?

The warm body hiring approach has decimated public opinion of careers in insurance, making the task of recruiting that much harder. Even worse, this hiring approach has the potential to destroy the reputation of your agency.

Your producers are the gears that drive your agency forward. They also represent your brand in the marketplace. It doesn't matter how hard you work to create a positive office environment and solid operations. Without the right people, you will struggle with growth, retention, and overall customer satisfaction. In other words, you will fail when it comes to everything that matters.

> ## ASA TIP
>
> We used to hire any person who walked through the door, and our turnover was ridiculous. Now we say, "Hire the best of the best, and forget the rest."

Hiring the next person who darkens your doorway is not a strategy—it's desperation. And desperation is not a sound approach for any business.

We are guilty of making desperation hires in the past. We used to bring aboard anyone who had an inkling of desire to give insurance a shot. What mattered most was that the person was interested in the first place. We would just take them as they came and figure out after we hired them what we needed to do to try to make them successful.

In working with agency owners across the country who come to our live events or enroll in our coaching programs, we have noticed a disturbing trend: most agency owners feel *lucky* when a decent candidate actually shows an interest in working for them.

Does that feel right to you?

We felt the same way, until we implemented the system detailed in this book. Today, we each operate with first-rate staff and almost no turnover.

THE NEVER-ENDING PLIGHT

It sounds so simple. "Just hire the right people." Anyone who has ever actually *tried* to hire good people might agree that the idea is far easier than the practice.

Hiring is the bane of every agency owner's existence. Hiring the right people—even the process of finding decent people to interview—is probably the toughest part of our job. And yet, the key to long-term success is having good people working for you and having great candidates in the queue *ready* to work for you.

Every industry faces this challenge. Good help is hard to find. Look around; it's easy to see what inferior hiring choices can do to a company.

However, what we have found is that bad hires often appear "bad" because they either received too little training or inadequate training. A lot of agency owners expect new hires to be high performers right away. It doesn't work like that, especially for those without any relevant experience. That leads us to a harsh truth:

Your team is a direct reflection of you.

Have you ever noticed when you watch a press conference after a big game, the winning coach will often say the reason they won was because *the players* implemented the playbook? *They* did exactly what they were supposed to do. *They* did everything that was asked of them.

However, if the team loses, the coach often takes responsibility. He or she will say, "I was the one who didn't successfully implement the game plan" or "I didn't coach my players well enough." Think about that the next time you complain about poor performances from your staff. If your players aren't playing well, you need to take a good look in the mirror.

When you hire without a well-defined process in place, what you end up with is rarely what you wanted. You may discover that your rising star who showed so much promise quickly turned into a high maintenance mistake. You may have also hired someone whose negative attitude and terrible work ethic poisoned the well in your agency. You might have gone against your better judgment and hired someone even though it just didn't feel right.

But you needed more agents, so you thought you'd get lucky and these hires would be exceptions to the rule and surprise you.

We've hired these gems, too. The key is to learn from each misstep so that you don't make it twice. And make sure to personally exemplify the actions and mindsets you want to see in your staff.

ALWAYS BE HIRING

One of the most famous depictions of the sales world is found in the movie *Glengarry Glen Ross*. Alec Baldwin's character, Blake, epitomizes the high-powered, zero-empathy, money-driven salesperson who gets what he wants through pressure, fear, and intimidation.

In one famous scene that coined a popular phrase, Blake told his salespeople they should, "A.B.C.—Always Be Closing."

Blake is right. Closing is a key step in the sales process. But there's another phrase that we believe is even more critical to your success: "A.B.H.—Always Be Hiring."

There will never come a time when you have assembled an unstoppable, permanent dream team. There is no such thing as picture-perfect hiring equilibrium within your agency. Commit to A.B.H.—and then use our hiring process to help you fill your roster with capable employees and keep it full.

If you are not constantly scouting for new talent, you'll end up making painful hiring mistakes. You will *desperately* need to fill a position, but there will be no good candidates in the queue, so you *desperately* hire the next person you interview.

Hiring under the gun impairs your judgment, which is why it's important to have a bench of players in the queue. Making recruiting part of your weekly activities will help you build up a database of solid salespeople for your bench.

REDSHIRTING PLAYERS

Continuously recruiting and having potential hires in the queue is known as *redshirting*. In sports, coaches keep redshirt players on the bench in order to build their skills for a future season. By building a reserve of solid candidates, you can have ample applicants at the ready when you need to fill a position.

Redshirting ensures you're never caught shorthanded if you lose a staff member. It's also the surest way to avoid becoming afflicted with warm body syndrome. Operating under the premise that *anybody* is better than *nobody* severely limits your agency's potential. Avoid this tactic at all costs.

Having plenty of players on deck also keeps your existing employees honest and is a great way to fuel healthy competition. When your staff sees you bringing in a steady stream of candidates, it acts as a silent and powerful motivator. On the other hand, if you are always scrambling to make last-minute hires, your existing agents may lose respect for their position.

HIRING PEOPLE FOR SPECIFIC ROLES

When we first decided to become agency owners, we were excited and optimistic. Who isn't excited in the honeymoon stage? We believed we could be successful—but like so many entrepreneurs, we had no idea actually how to do that.

That led to utilizing strategies that backfired. For example, in the beginning we neglected to assign specific roles to anyone. The unspoken philosophy in our agencies was, "Whoever is in the office and doesn't have a bagel in their hand, answer the phone and handle it."

> **ASA TIP**
>
> Never count on new hires to be the solution to an empty position. Some people talk a good game, but can they deliver? And will they even show up on the first day? You never know!

We expected every person to wear every hat. Everyone answered the phone, dealt with customer service issues, and did paperwork. The biggest problem with this strategy was that every person was also expected to sell. That was an error that cost us dearly during the first few years.

Each person has specific gifts and talents. Your job as a leader is to put people into positions where they can flourish. You must place employees in their wheelhouse and allow them to perform tasks that best suit them.

If you want to hire great people who fit with you and your existing team, you've got to follow a specific process. Find the absolute best staff to help you carry out your vision. This, like anything else, is done best with a proven system.

THE REAL COST OF A BAD HIRE

Bad hires can cause devastating loss to a business, loss that is almost incalculable. The wrong hire can be a momentum destroyer. Desperation hires have been known to crush morale. They can also cause rifts among the team that may never be repaired.

These things and more end up costing you a lot of money. According to CareerBuilder.com, 66 percent of U.S. employers reported their company was adversely affected by at least one bad hire in the past year. As many as 41 percent of those surveyed estimated that each bad hire cost them $25,000 in lost revenue, while 27 percent say that number is closer to $50,000.[1]

Your salespeople/agents are the most expensive staff members to recruit and replace. For this reason, we're going to focus on the best hiring practices for agents. Let's start by looking at some of the major impacts of the wrong agent hire:

Reduced Revenue. One hiring mistake can hurt everyone's income. If you have to spend time trying to "fix" someone, you lose some of your own earning time. If you assign a top performer to help, his or her production suffers. Someone who has one foot out the door won't treat current accounts or prospects properly, which leads to the loss of current and potential business.

---

1 Gillet, Rachel. "How Much a Bad Hire Will Actually Cost You." *Fast Money*, April 2014, online edition.

Lost Productivity. Bad hires definitely won't produce what you expect. The wrong hire burns through good leads that could have led to more business. Your productivity will also be compromised, as well as that of anyone who works with or helps train this person.

Lost Recruiting Time and Cost. Not only are you out the time and expense it took you to recruit and train this agent, but now you have to take the time to find, recruit, and train another person to take his or her place. How much is your time really worth? For us, that time is worth a lot, and we'd rather not waste it.

Weakened Employee Morale. The wrong agents can infect other agents with their toxic attitude. Your hardworking agents may also resent the amount of time you spend trying to salvage a bad egg. That can erode trust and team cohesion.

There are plenty of other ways a bad hire can destroy an agency, but you *can* avoid these expensive mistakes. There is a better way. We run some of the highest performing agencies in the country—and one of the cornerstones of that success is our hiring process.

Over the next few chapters, we're going to share with you the hiring principles and the ten-step process that changed the path of our businesses and could turn your career and your agency into a similar success story.

Find the Right Candidates

Most businesses struggle with finding salespeople who possess the right attitude, work ethic, and skills to be successful. Some believe such superstars don't exist anymore, or at least are on their way to extinction.

If you've ever felt that way, you are not alone. After a lot of turnover and frustration, we discovered that there are still plenty of good, even *great* candidates out there. You simply have to know what to look for and how to find them.

The problem for most agencies is that they expend their effort on the wrong end of the process. Many agency owners spend most of their time putting out the fires of their most high-maintenance employees or trying to turn low performers into high performers.

This is completely backwards.

The emphasis should be on recruiting, interviewing, hiring, and onboarding. If you've ever wondered how some agencies seem to be effortlessly functioning, *that* is their secret. There is tremendous effort, but the effort comes during the recruitment process, not after.

Let's start with the types of candidates you want to target.

TALENT VERSUS EXPERIENCE

In a perfect world, you can have it all. You can have your cake and eat it, too. You can have fries *and* onion rings. There are always free refills. The light stays green. You can always hire people with sales experience *and* talent who are coachable and have a commitment to excellence.

But we don't live in a perfect world. There aren't too many employees who have it all. It often comes down to the choice between sales experience and natural talent. Which do you choose?

In the battle between experience and talent, you're always better off choosing talent.

The tendency is to look for salespeople from within the industry—but while hiring veteran agents may seem like a plug-and-play solution, this is often far from the truth.

Experienced candidates often have preconceived notions about the way an insurance agency should be run. And, if we're honest, most of us will admit that the majority of insurance agencies are, at best, mediocre operations. That means an experienced candidate more than likely worked at a mediocre agency.

Do you really want someone in your office who expects things to be average?

You're going to have a difficult time creating a *top* agency by hiring only people who have worked in *typical* agencies, particularly if they worked there for an extended period of time.

Talent is far more desirable than experience. If you have a soccer team and your goalie gets injured, you don't go out and hire a new goalie simply if he or she has been a goalie before and knows the rules. You go out and find someone who has the raw talent to play the position well—and then you *teach* him or her the right way to play.

If you hire a new agent who has talent, inherent ability, and all the intangibles necessary to do the job, you can *teach* them the insurance side.

The vernacular and information can be learned, but you can't teach potential, and you can't instill those intangibles that only great salespeople possess.

If you are not sure which direction to take, step outside the résumé and look for things that can't be properly expressed on a piece of paper. A solid work ethic, a good dose of humility, and the ability to remain coachable can go a long way in this industry. Find someone who sets personal goals and strives hard to achieve them.

HIGH PERFORMERS

It may seem obvious, but your focus must be on finding high performers. Bring people aboard who believe they will shine and can prove it during the interview process.

This type of candidate can be difficult to identify, especially in the beginning of your recruiting efforts. This is why you should invest in a testing system that can help you separate the high performers from the rest. (We'll cover behavioral and personality assessments in the next chapter.)

ASA TIP

While trusting your gut is always a part of the hiring process, it should never be the *only* way you make hiring decisions.

Aside from skill and personality assessments, you should also pay close attention to how they performed in their previous positions. If they were in cell phone sales, check their performance. How much did they sell, and how did they rank among other salespeople? If they were consistently among the top in their company or were given awards or bonuses for their ability to sell, chances are you have a high performer.

It is important to note that high achievers and mediocre performers typically don't get along well. If you're trying to build a team of winners, you must focus on bringing in high performers for the sake of everyone on your team.

Does that mean you should only hire superstars? As great as that would be, there can only be one #1 performer, which means you need a solid team playing alongside the top performers. As long as you have people who give you their best, remain coachable, and have a desire to succeed, that's all you can ask for.

What is the key to assembling the right mix of players? Your hiring process will determine whether you have a group of winners, a group of average people, or an unhealthy mix that may lead to conflict down the road.

Adopting a proven hiring formula is huge. Then you create a culture where agents are required to continue earning their place on the team.

It's not luck. It's not fate.

It hinges on implementing a proven hiring process.

NATURAL BORN SALESPEOPLE

It's imperative that you seek out and hire top-notch salespeople. While effective sales techniques can absolutely be learned, there are some people who are naturally more gifted at selling in less-than-ideal environments. These top talents have specific personality traits and skills that allow them to sell almost anything.

We've all met people who succeed in whatever they do—like they were born to win. When you add people like that to your organization, you have to go out of your way to make them fail. No matter how many obstacles are placed in front of them, they will find a way to sell. Once you learn how to identify and attract top performers, you will experience explosive growth.

One of the best books about hiring is *The Ultimate Sales Machine* by corporate trainer and strategic consultant Chet Holmes. Chet understands what makes natural born salespeople tick because he is one of them.

While working under Charlie Monger, one of Warren Buffett's most trusted partners, Chet doubled the sales in a division of a billion-dollar company three years in a row. Imagine what your business would look like if you doubled sales in one year. Now imagine doing it two more times.

Experience, age, and background all run a distant second to one thing—personality. Top salespeople have a certain personality. When you market to them and then interview them, everything you do has to speak to that personality.

Learn to identify top performers quickly, because you won't find them very often. From our experience, we've found that candidates with the right personality make up less than 10 percent of the candidate pool.

It's not easy to find these people, but anything worth having is never easy. You can take the path of *least* resistance and get the *least* results, or you can take the unbeaten path to massive growth and an abundance of new business.

HIDDEN SALES GEMS

If you want the best, you must know where to look. This generally starts with a well-written, well-placed ad. However, because the Internet has become polluted with low-quality, churn-and-burn type job postings that are filled with false promises, you may find success by thinking outside the box.

One of the best ways to keep your employee pipeline full of potential is to find people who are not necessarily looking for work at the moment. We call them "hidden sales gems." These are people who work at places like the mall, cell phone stores, and rental car companies.

These types of employees work lots of hours in some sort of sales position that requires them to dress professionally and deal with the public. Such people are more likely to have the talents and abilities you want.

Some of our most valuable assets wouldn't have become part of our teams if we didn't adhere to the A.B.H. philosophy. The next time you're in any type of retail establishment, observe the employees. You may find your agency's next top performer.

NETWORKING FOR ANOTHER KIND OF LEAD

There are many advantages to networking—and most people agree it's a great way to find more business.

It's also a great way to find new salespeople.

To maximize your networking efforts, make your needs known to as many people as possible. Tell members of your professional network that you are looking to fill a sales position. Be clear about the job and provide a brief list of the skills or talents required. Then get the word out by emailing and connecting to those in your network through LinkedIn and other online communities.

Don't neglect the importance of person-to-person conversations with centers of influence (COIs) in your network. Buy them coffee, take them to lunch, and talk to them about your agency and the kind of people you want. Not only will the COIs in your network be able to refer candidates to you directly, but they might also provide you with new contacts to help you widen your search radius.

Because your professional network is such a valuable resource for your recruiting efforts, invest the time to keep the connections alive, and to expand them.

Another source for recruits is your client base. This referral group has the benefit of personal experience as buyers. Ask your clients if they have met any salespeople recently who stand out. There is really no better measure of a salesperson's performance than the way in which they service their current customers.

A well-written, well-placed ad—which is the first step in our hiring process that starts in the next chapter—is an essential part of your recruiting efforts. But you should cast an even wider net by using these outside-the-box recruiting techniques to ensure you have an overflowing candidate queue at all times.

Make Great
First Impressions

O ver the next few chapters, we are going to walk through the ten steps of our proven and tested hiring process. When used properly, this system will transform your agency faster than any other change you can make.

This process should be constantly in use, and once you set this process in motion, it should stay in motion!

Remember, A.B.H.—always be hiring.

STEP 1: PLACE AN AD

Top performing sales professionals are looking for opportunities to excel. They're not looking for a high guaranteed income—those don't exist in pure sales positions anyway—but they do want the possibility of high commissions. The wording of your ad is critical to convey the right message.

What to Say

Your ad must highlight possibilities of what *could be* in your agency. If you present the ad as an hourly position, as in, "This job pays $12 to $15 per hour, plus commission," that will not attract hungry, top performers.

The best ads speak to the highest possibility. What is the most someone can make in your agency in the first year? Just don't make a number up to sound more appealing. Always be real and authentic.

Your ad must convey that a sizable income is within reach. That's how you attract star salespeople; they know they've got what it takes to sell, and they are just looking for the right opportunity that will allow them to maximize their potential.

To attract the most desireable agents, you must write a job advertisement, not a job description. There is a distinct difference. A job description does just that—it describes the duties of the role. Details are important, but an ad's primary purpose is to get the right people to feel compelled to apply.

You must speak to the potential of the job and also include a sense of your agency's culture and mission. Why do you think your agency is such a great place to work? Why is a sales position in your agency something to be sought after?

Include a short summary of what your agency values most, and be sure *not* to use terms such as "sales ninja" or "rock star" since phrases like those do not convey the true professionalism and importance of the job. Remember that in today's low unemployment market conditions, you may want to contact everyone who applies. It's a competitive job market, so follow up on every opportunity.

Where to Advertise

A common mistake many agencies make is using only the most popular job boards. While a giant online job board may attract millions of visitors, it might not always attract the most serious, qualified candidates. Use the most well-known job websites to widen your reach, but be aware of their limitations.

For the insurance industry, Ideal Traits (IdealTraits.com) is a great place to start advertising. Ideal Traits empowers you with templates designed to provide maximum exposure and makes it easy for those who are new to writing ads.

After you write the ad, Ideal Traits will create a professionally branded landing page that is unique to your agency. This allows everything you publish to have a consistent look and message. Once the ad is complete, you can easily share your job with all major social networks.

Finally, Ideal Traits will post your job with their integrated online partners. You can post to their free job boards, or boost visibility with paid services like Indeed.com and drive local job seekers to your unique, branded landing page.

If you decide you would rather use another service or job posting website, the same rules apply. Make sure that the material you publicize has a consistent tone and feel.

After you post your ad, regularly search for new hires (A.B.H.!). Once this process is in motion, you must work to keep it in motion. Make it your goal to interview at least one person per week, room on the roster or not, to build up your agency's bench of redshirts.

STEP 2: PHONE PRE-INTERVIEW

The phone-based pre-interview should be short and to the point—the goal being to weed out the bad fits before they spend another second in the process.

The call should take no longer than ten minutes, and it should be scripted. A script serves two purposes: First, it gives you a universal set of questions to ask every applicant. Second, it takes emotion out of the interview and replaces it with logic. Here are some questions we use:

- Why do you feel you would be a good fit?
- Tell me why you think you would enjoy a commission-based position over an hourly or salaried position.

Your goal in the pre-interview is to make a logical decision about whether the candidate has enough potential to continue. As hard as it may be after a great conversation, avoid the temptation to think you just found the next great top performing agent. Making assumptions too early in the process skews your interpretation of everything he or she says after that initial impression.

A good first impression doesn't close the deal; it just moves a candidate to the next step.

STEP 3: PERSONALITY ASSESSMENT

Once you use Ideal Traits to spread the word about the job, you can use it to conduct a personality assessment. This step will save you tons of time, and will go a long way toward singling out potential top achievers.

The Ideal Traits Assessment is a personality profile evaluation that every candidate who is interested in the position must take. The test is based on a proven assessment used by over 3,500 agents across the country and counting. Ideal Traits looks at a candidate's quantitative values of drive and motivation, persuasive ability, thoroughness and compliance, and structure and routine.

This step helps you narrow the field down to those who have the highest probability of success and can eliminate as many as 80 percent of your in-person interviews, which saves you an incredible amount of time and money.

After passing the pre-interview, your potential candidates will receive a link to take a four-part assessment. Here is a breakdown of each part:

1. An application where they fill out their work history and upload their résumé.
2. A short-answer section where they answer five questions about why they feel they would be right for the position.
3. A problem-solving section, which becomes a great differentiator when deciding between two similar candidates. When in doubt, hire the better problem solver.
4. The assessment, which is a useful tool that gives you an idea of how they react under pressure, how they see themselves, and how others perceive them.

We ask applicants to take the test in one of our offices. This gives us a truer depiction of who they are, and it also ensures that they are the ones who are actually taking the test.

Always review the results of the assessment *before* conducting the in-person interview. People can interview well and fool you. We've all hired the wrong people who interviewed far better than they scored on the test. Don't make that mistake.

Ideal Traits gives you the tools you need to make an educated decision based on defined skill sets and behaviors rather than on gut feelings and emotions. It ensures you are talking to a candidate who is well equipped to be an asset to your agency.

ASA TIP

Something we have realized over 20+ years of sales management is this—you just can't teach motivation! Either they have it or they don't. Make that type of attitude a requirement, not something you try to teach. Because you can't.

In our agencies, we hire candidates who score high in the areas of motivation and drive and who show they have good persuasion skills. In the long run, they will require less management and motivation than others to reach goals because they are naturally self-motivated, self-inspired, and enjoy challenges.

Online sales assessments take the uncertainty out of hiring by determining specific attributes required for success in that position, then allowing you to compare candidates objectively against that criteria.

Once you start using a personality and behavior assessment tool, you'll wonder how you ever hired without one. Research the options available and find the one that works best for you; it will save you from wasting days or even weeks in the hiring process with a candidate who is simply not right for the position.

Get Face-to-Face

A t this point in the hiring process, every candidate should have taken a personality assessment. Don't take your review of those results lightly. Carefully review the results, looking for the key things top performers possess.

Once you determine you have a candidate worthy of the next step, invite him or her in for the face-to-face interview.

STEP 4: IN-PERSON INTERVIEW

You already know your applicant has the basic tools and the right personality needed to perform at a high level. The in-person interview is your chance to see some of those ideal traits in action.

Allow an hour for the interview. Good ones will last at least that long; bad ones will be over much sooner. An hour is a big commitment, but applicants who made it to this stage have earned it. They took initiative and called your office to indicate interest in the position. They passed the pre-interview and scored well on the assessment.

You are now willing to invest an hour of your own time because you know these candidates have the potential to be great salespeople. They have it within them; they are driven; they are motivated; they have talent. Now it's time to find out if everything else fits.

The interview should ideally be with you, but you could also choose a trusted person within your agency. During in-person interviews, watch for three main things:

1. **Can they open up?** Agents must be personable and able to engage in friendly, back-and-forth conversation.
2. **How do you feel when they talk to you?** Do they convey a feeling of trust? Do you find yourself bored by a monotone voice or struggling to keep up with a rambling story, or do you find yourself interested in what they are saying and energized by their presence?
3. **Can they wow you when they speak?** Do their answers impress you, or do they leave you wondering how they scored so well on the assessment? Would you buy something they were selling?

Keep those three questions in mind as we discuss the eight elements of an effective candidate interview:

1. Start with brief, casual questions.

Since this may be the start of a long relationship, begin with a few icebreakers to loosen up the applicant and lighten the mood. Say something like, "Tell me about yourself, something that's not on your résumé," or "Tell me something that other people admire about you." Get the interviewee talking.

Lightly dig into their past, with the intention of finding out if they've ever been in sales before, and more specifically, in insurance sales.

Hiring someone with insurance sales experience is risky. They may come with bad habits that are hard to break. If they've been away from the industry long enough, they may have forgotten why they left. You don't want them to reminisce about the "good times" at their last sales job, only to quit after you've spent lots of time and money hiring and onboarding them.

2. Ask a series of probing, open-ended questions.

After you break the ice, the general line of questioning shouldn't fluctuate much. Ideally, you should ask the same questions to all candidates for consistency and comparison. Without a question plan, you risk having the conversation go off-topic or losing control of the interview. Here are some good questions:

- What are a few of your greatest work-related contributions?
- Outside of work, where do you spend most of your time?
- What's most important to you in your next position?
- What prompted you to send us your résumé?
- What do you know about the insurance industry?
- When I call your references, what are they going to say about you other than you are a hard worker?
- What did you like most or least about your last position?
- When was the last time you did something nice for someone?
- What kind of career path are you looking for?

Although these questions are generic, you can use them as a transition to more targeted, open-ended questions that will be based on the responses you receive.

For instance, you could start out with, "Outside of work, where do you spend most of your time?" Then follow up with an influence question like, "It sounds like you spend a lot of your time assisting your high school club. How do you plan on leveraging that time to bring in additional sales to the agency?"

The open-ended approach works with job-specific questions as well. During the interview, let them know that this career requires a lot of networking and making outbound calls. Instead of leading them with a question like, "Do you think you could be an efficient telemarketer?" ask them, "Tell me how you feel about outbound sales calls."

For a more specific answer, you could ask, "What in particular excites you about constantly chasing new business and selling?"

By refining your open-ended questions, your candidate's answers will allow you to separate the good from the bad. Stick to a game plan. Ask only open-ended questions in your next interview. The goal is for the candidate to do most of the talking.

Avoid closed-ended questions such as, "Do you feel you're a hard worker?" Questions that require only a yes or no answer do not reveal enough about what makes the candidate tick.

Top salespeople will run with open-ended questions. They'll open up. It will feel like you've known them forever. They'll talk about their family; they'll talk about their background.

Top salespeople are simply great at connecting.

The best agents are excellent relationship builders. Inherent within the best relationships is *trust*—and that trust is a key to accelerated growth. So, make sure they've got what it takes to cultivate relationships and become someone your customers can trust.

3. Walk through the résumé.

Next, briefly walk through their résumé. Spend a minute or two talking about each place they worked. It's important to determine a few key things about each job:

1. Find out why they chose that job.
2. Find out why they left. Was it on good terms or were they fired for non-performance or another major issue?
3. What were their measurable successes? Did they meet quotas, meet or exceed expectations, or create quantifiable results that speak to their tenacity, work ethic, and talent?

The résumé's main purpose is to give you a list of the places they worked so you can dig into their past performances. It doesn't matter whether the positions were sales related—every job has quantifiable measures of success you can use to determine what you need to know.

4. Apply pressure.

In any sales role, pressure permeates. You need to know how a person will react in environments filled with pressure. Here is one way we turn up the heat. Look interviewees in the eyes and say:

> "Your interview has been great so far. Your résumé is fantastic. I really appreciate you coming in, but I hire top performers for a living. That's what I do, and frankly I don't think you're the kind of sales professional I'm looking for."

Then shut up and wait; the next thing out of their mouth will reveal what you need to know. Some candidates may think the interview is over and not even attempt to defend themselves. Others may become indignant or offended. The best candidates will respectfully tell you that you are wrong about them without flinching.

Another statement that applies pressure is, "Tell me why I shouldn't hire you."

This will stop people in their tracks because it's not a typical interview question. It forces them to think on their feet and be spontaneous.

You might also ask, "If you could change one thing about yourself, what would it be?" The point is to create an environment where they have to think on their toes. Since a sales career is challenging and constantly evolving, the job interview should be, too.

Some agency owners may find that it works better to wait until later in the process to apply this kind of pressure. Whether you choose to use this technique now or later, you'll find it highly effective at revealing the amount of fight in a candidate.

5. Convey that this is a career, not a job.

It is critical to impress upon applicants that you are discussing a career with them, not a résumé filler. You are not looking to be a stepping-stone for someone to use to land another job. You need career-minded people who desire to be successful and who want to run an agency for you one day.

You can tell a lot about people by how they react to the idea that a sales position is a career, not just a job. Also, look for telltale signs that they will jump ship. Do they live an hour and a half away from the office? That's not going to work. A three-hour round-trip commute on top of a nine- or ten-hour workday is simply not sustainable.

Make sure they understand that you are not their boss. If you hire them, you'll become their coach and mentor. Bosses micromanage, while coaches and mentors help people succeed. Coaches find what makes people better, and they help their team rise to higher levels.

You are looking for self-motivated people who don't need to be micromanaged. At the same time, you need them to be coachable without becoming defensive. They must be able to come to work every day with the same great attitude they displayed during the interview process.

Don't think this type of candidate exists? If not, then you haven't interviewed any top performers yet.

6. Convey a little healthy fear.

Most agency owners will admit that their hiring philosophy is, "If they actually want to sell, they're hired!" This is the same mindset that has caused the insurance sector to be marred by high turnover. It results in an overall lack of quality that does not represent the incredible products and solutions our industry has to offer.

That is why we are proposing such a radically different view of hiring.

We give candidates every reason to think the position may not work for them. We paint a truthful picture of the long road ahead, because we want only those who have the self-confidence to take on the challenge, overcome objections, and sell themselves to us.

If a tough conversation about the hardships of a sales career sends a candidate running, then congratulations! You were just handed a gift. That person would have gotten three months into the job and jumped ship, landing you back at square one.

Don't be afraid to get a little uncomfortable making them a little uncomfortable. Ask tough questions like:

- What did you not like about your last sales manager?
- What would you have changed about your last job?
- Is there anything that could have kept you working at your previous company?
- How do you actively plan to achieve your goals over the next five years?
- What do you not like about working?

If you really want to test their grit, ask them to sell you something that is sitting on your desk. It could be a stapler, a pen, a laptop, anything. Put them on the spot and ask them to sell that item to you.

Being so uncompromising in your hiring process will cause many applicants to fall short, which may hinder your ability to cultivate that bench of prospective employees you need.

The solution? A.B.H.!

Wherever you go, everyone should know what you do. If you see people who are really great at their jobs, hand them your business card and tell them that you're always hiring sharp people like them. Seek out the hidden sales gems. Find the diamonds in the rough. They *are* out there.

7. Set clear expectations.

Throughout the interview, clearly convey the attributes that you expect to see in all team members. Here are the types of expectations we set with every potential new hire:

i. **Always have a great attitude.** This is easy to say you'll do, but hard to execute. The key is to find people who can have a great attitude after a big win and after a devastating loss.

ii. **Be coachable.** No matter how good they think they are, they can always improve. Do they have the right mix of humility and confidence?

iii. **Know what you don't know.** We've hired people with lots of experience who think they already know the best way to do everything. You need them to do it your way and to admit that they don't know it all.

iv. **Take initiative to be a student of your craft.** They say it takes 10,000 dedicated hours to become great at anything. Agents must be students of their craft and strive to become better versions of themselves. Always be learning and improving.

8. Manage expectations.

At the end of the in-person interview, your applicants may be feeling a little overwhelmed. That's good! You want the decision to work for you to be made after careful deliberation and with a full awareness of the pros and the cons.

Let them know what to expect next. Give them an approximate time frame in which you will contact them to either thank them for their time or ask them to move on to the next stage.

STEP 5: STAFF INTERVIEW

The one-on-one interview was a great start. It provided you key insights into the applicant, but the work is not over. If the first interview went well, ask the candidate to come back for the staff interview. For a more streamlined approach, you could conduct the staff interview on the same day as the one-on-one interview.

The staff interview consists of one to three staff people, including at least one manager and another person who works in the position for which the candidate is applying. The most tenured agent, sales manager, or manager for that location should conduct the group interview.

If you conducted the one-on-one interview, you should not be in the room for this one. Once the staff interview begins, step out of the room, close the door, and allow the candidate to speak freely and in confidence to the group.

STEP 5

> **ASA TIP**
>
> Don't oversell the position. It's important to give the candidate the most accurate vision as to what it's actually like to work in your agency.

The people who will be working shoulder-to-shoulder with candidates should have some sort of involvement in their hiring. By involving the staff in the process, they have some ownership in the decision.

Getting staff members involved develops a sense of cohesion and fosters a helpful team spirit. It's nice to know they had some influence in that person being hired. Don't underestimate how huge this is. An empowered, appreciated staff is a productive staff.

Encourage candidates to ask your team any questions they want, even sensitive ones, such as:

- "What's your boss like?"
- "How do you get paid?"
- "Do you really like it here?"
- "What's this atmosphere like when the owner isn't around?"

The staff interview should only last about 30 minutes, but this is plenty of time for candidates to connect with the team and get a better feel for the environment. The more they know about the position and the agency, the better.

After the group interview, listen to your team's assessment of the candidate. This potential hire will be working closely with them, so if they like the new team member, this leads to a much higher probability of success. If your staff has issues with the candidate from the start, pay attention. If trusted employees see problems during the interview, that candidate is not going to be the right fit.

STEP 6: CHECK REFERENCES

You may be tempted to skip this next step. But don't. Check references! We have learned that candidates' behavior at a previous employer is indicative of their future behavior.

"Oh, but they've changed!"

Yeah, we doubt it.

Talk to any employer, owner, manager, or supervisor who used to oversee them. Those past leaders will give you the best insight into how candidates will act in the future.

If they were in a sales position before and underperformed, that's a huge red flag. If they couldn't sell cell phones, houses, or even shoes, what makes you think they can sell insurance?

Don't even bother with personal references. You should never let what a candidate's best friend or aunt says about them have any sway in your opinion. Target former bosses and managers.

When you call, ask tough questions and don't sugarcoat. Get to the heart of any issues quickly and efficiently. Ask enough detailed questions to determine that the listed reference really knows the candidate. This is especially important to ensure that what the person put on his or her application was truthful.

Checking references serves one more useful purpose. It gives candidates time to go home and think about the opportunity. In fact, we ask all candidates to undergo a three-day contemplation period.

Encourage applicants to talk to their friends and family about the job during this time. Since a lot of people outside the industry are prone to view sales positions in a less-than-desirable light, they're going to get some negative input—and that's exactly what you want.

If someone else's negative opinion can so easily dissuade a candidate, you don't want that person to work for you anyway.

Make sure you have checked all references so you know whether or not you want to continue the process if and when they decide to move forward.

If they are still interested in the position after speaking with friends and family, you know they heard plenty of skepticism and doubt but still want to move forward.

That's a good sign.

Now it's on to the proving grounds.

Enter the
Proving Grounds

This next step is a lot like Major League tryouts. You've scouted them, you've witnessed their talent, and you feel they could be a great fit on the team.

But you won't really know until you see them in action.

STEP 7: EXTENDED INTERVIEW/JOB SHADOW

If all goes well, it's time to bring them in for a less formal meeting. This next step will get them directly involved with their new potential teammates. It's a great time to start going over the basics of the position.

In the past, we hired some of the best interviewees on the spot. This knee-jerk decision backfired on us so many times that we finally realized a few more steps are needed in between conducting a great in-person interview and officially hiring them.

We've hired people who blew us away during the interview but failed miserably with even the most basic tasks once they were in the office. Some people can't perform a Google search or navigate a computer. Hard to believe, but it's true. We've watched these candidates while scratching our heads and thinking, "Who is this person, and what did he do with the remarkable candidate from the interview?"

The extended interview helps you avoid those head-scratching moments. It allows you to determine whether or not candidates can handle some of the basic duties of the position.

Have candidates come into the office for a few hours, up to a full day. Assign them some simple tasks to perform on the computer or a few straightforward operational duties within the office. See how well they handle everyday tasks. It is important to note that if a candidate does any work for you, and especially if the candidate picks up the phone and speaks with any customers or prospective customers or listens in on a call, you are required to pay them.

Don't prep current team members for these extended interviews. Let them be themselves. If your employees have negative things to say or feel the need to complain about something, give them space to do so.

It's best for the environment to mirror the actual working conditions and day-to-day operations of your agency as much as possible.

You can also use this time to test their basic phone and sales skills through role-playing. Have an agent play the part of the prospect on the other end of the phone. Go through a series of scenarios and see how easily this person can build rapport, overcome objections, use assumptive closes, and demonstrate other sales skills.

The calls will give you a glimpse into how new hires will present themselves on the phone, which is where they'll spend a great deal of their time. You're not looking for perfection in this exercise. You simply want to assess their current skill level and determine if they are coachable and eager to learn the trade.

Finally, they should spend the remainder of the day shadowing a top agent. Allow candidates to watch one of your best performers—what they do on a daily basis and how they handle phone and in-person presentations.

The longer they stay at the office, the better. The more they observe and experience, the more prepared they will be after they're hired.

Whatever you do, be careful not to present the "first date" version of the agency. Don't gloss over imperfections. Present it for what it is, good and bad. This transparency helps to safeguard against new hires getting scared off after some water cooler talk a few weeks into the job.

It also prevents you from making hires under insincere pretenses. If new hires encounter something vastly different from what they were anticipating after they start, they'll think, "Hey! This is *not* what I was expecting."

When they start down that road of thought, there's almost no going back.

This is also a good time to turn up the pressure if you didn't already do that earlier in the process. You can say something like, "Frankly, I'm just not sure you're the person for this position."

Are they going to cave in or fight back? Their answer will reveal much about the type of salesperson and representative they will be for your agency.

With the extended interview day under your belts, both you and they will have a much better idea about whether this is the career for them. It may have unearthed some things that stop the process in its tracks on either end. If so, it was worth one day to expose that before any more time or money was spent.

STEP 8: LICENSING

If the shadowing day was a success, it's time to move to the next step: the licensing process. While we prefer candidates with no prior experience as insurance agents, we certainly do want them to have a license.

There are many things that can go wrong between hiring and licensing, which is why you should require new agents to get the appropriate license *prior* to starting. Depending on where you live, this process can take anywhere from ten days to a month. Ideally, this is something you have already highlighted at the start of the process, so there is no surprise when candidates reach this phase.

Candidates should obtain their licenses before you hire them for two main reasons:

1. If you hire someone and start the training and onboarding process before they are licensed, there's a good chance they will not pass the test or quit before they are ever licensed.
2. It serves as another assessment. Are they willing and able to independently study, pay for, and acquire their license without you holding their hand?

Step eight makes for a great separator among candidates. It requires commitment on the candidates' part by asking them to spend money prior to getting hired. It also displays their level of initiative and confidence. As a bonus, the studying required to pass the exam gives them great foundational knowledge at the outset.

Candidates who are not willing to spend time and money on licensing will easily walk away. If they shrink back when faced with the prospect of getting licensed, it's not likely they'd have been able to succeed in this business anyway.

Touch base and check in on their progress during the testing period. Sometimes, candidates will fail the exam several times. In fact, some of our most highly decorated salespeople failed multiple times.

If they fail one or more times, let them know that this is normal and even expected. Reassure them that some of the most successful agents and agency owners in the business failed the test numerous times. Start showing them what real support looks and feels like from their leader and coach. Ask them to assess where they think they are missing the mark and encourage them to study and try again.

By trying again, they display relentless determination that will translate into a tremendous drive to succeed. If a candidate shows that much persistence in getting the job (not to mention the willingness to pay to take the test more than once), imagine how persistently that agent will go after a sale.

Those are the kinds of people you want on your staff, and this process is what will reveal them to you.

We recommend that you do not pay candidates for the time they spend preparing for the test. This should be something they do on their own. (Note: You can choose to reimburse them for some or all of the testing costs.)

The key is to help them understand that the time and dollars it will take to become licensed is truly an investment in themselves.

How many people invest $100,000 or more to go to college for years, only to get a job making $40,000 to $50,000 a year? Help them see that investing a few weeks of their time and a few hundred dollars will provide them with the opportunity to generate a six-figure income.

For many, that's a better investment than a college degree.

If prospective agents are not willing to invest in themselves to gain access to a career that can make them a lot of money, the job is not for them.

At the end of step eight, your candidates have taken initiative and impressed you in person. They have also proven that they possess the attributes of a successful salesperson and are willing to invest in themselves. They took action to get their license, proving they want the position and are willing to make sacrifices to get there.

Now they are on the home stretch.

STEP 9: LEAD COLLECTION

The next step is the post-licensing declaration page ("dec page") and lead collection. Since they are now licensed, they can interact with customers. In fact, they can do everything except bind (you can register them for binding authority as soon as the class is available).

During this step, candidates must reach certain goals you set for them. You can choose to set goals for the number of calls they make, the number of appointments they set, the amount of new business they are able to bring in during that time, or all of the above.

We also recommend you require two specific things from candidates (if these are applicable to your agency):

1. Collect Dec Pages.

Ask all candidates to collect a certain number of dec pages. A dec page is the first page of a customer's policy summarizing their coverage and coverage levels. You collect copies of prospective customers' dec pages when providing a quote on insurance.

Requiring candidates to collect a certain number of these pages (we use a benchmark of 50 pages) allows them to experience what it feels like to ask for business. It will also give them their first taste of rejection, since not all prospects will be willing to hand over copies of their dec pages.

That failure is just as important as the successes. It will give them another opportunity to know what it feels like to be a licensed sales representative for your agency. You may choose to incentivize the dec page collection by giving them $10 per page collected. This will put some money in their pockets and help offset the cost of testing.

> **ASA TIP**
>
> You must question any candidate who isn't willing to collect dec pages and leads, since a primary focus of their new selling career will involve convincing others to get a quote.

The point is to set your new hires up to succeed by helping them gain momentum. If they start with 50 dec pages from friends and family in hand, they will more than likely have a high close rate during their first month—and that will boost their confidence.

Imagine having two new hires start on the same day. One walks in with 50 dec pages, and the other walks in with none. Which would you consider the better candidate?

2. Bring in New Leads.

The final requirement is for candidates to produce at least 25 new leads. Since a healthy pipeline is the backbone of our business, you must be confident that new agents are able to collect leads to add to their prospect pool. You don't want order takers—you want rainmakers. Make sure they can get leads from the start.

Clearly explain all the expectations and define the standards in every phase of the hiring process. Make it abundantly clear what you are looking for and what is going to be expected of them. There should be no surprises.

After steps one through nine are complete, you must ask yourself, "Is this person a career-oriented rainmaker or a good candidate who is just not the right fit?"

Your answer leads you to the moment of truth.

STEP 10: HIRING AND ONBOARDING

What a ride it's been up to this tenth and final step! If a candidate has reached this point, let's review their journey:

1. They were looking for a new career and responded to your ad. Or you sought them out or were given their name as a referral.
2. They sounded sharp and well-spoken during a brief, scripted phone conversation.
3. They passed a personality and behavioral assessment.
4. They wowed you during the in-person interview.
5. They impressed other members of your staff during the staff interview.
6. They contemplated the position while you checked their references.
7. They had a successful day of observation and shadowing.
8. They passed their licensing test.
9. They collected dec page and leads, proved they were coachable, and met all of the targets you set for them.

Now you must decide:

Should they stay or should they go?

If they succeeded in all nine previous steps, then congrats! Candidates who have done so much to prove their worth are much more likely to be the types of assets we need in our agencies. To get through all these steps to being hired is an accomplishment in and of itself.

You should be excited to have such a dedicated new hire. Be sure to share that enthusiasm with them and the rest of the staff. Our agencies are like our second families. It's important that we all feel like a team, cheer for each other, and get along, especially since we spend more time with our work families than with our actual families.

THE FINAL TEST

Once you offer the position and they accept, it's time to begin the next phase: training and onboarding.

The training process can be viewed as a probationary period that lasts 90 days, during which they are required to produce a specified amount of new business. Whatever targets you select, they must be: 1) realistic, 2) clearly defined, and 3) easily measured.

As long as new hires reach their objectives each week, their employment continues on during the probationary period. If they reach their goals for month two, then they are eligible to continue on to month three. Once they reach month three's targets, you can consider them a full-time team member.

There are multiple ways to structure training during their 90-day probationary period and beyond. Whatever you decide to use, create a training manual that contains all of your processes to ensure uniformity in the process.

To receive a free copy of the training manual we use for onboarding and training, please visit: agencysalesacademy.com/growth.

Make sure new hires know exactly what to anticipate during the trial period. Communicate with them from day one what you expect, by when you expect it, and why you expect it.

If you discover that new agents seem to need extreme hand holding and constant corrections, you can be thankful you built in that probationary period! They can move on and find a position better suited to them, and you can feel relieved that you dodged a bullet.

On the other hand, the best agents will take the initiative and beat the targets you set for them.

Although basic selling principles remain the same no matter what you sell, what works for one person may not always work for another. Allow new hires to see and hear different perspectives on the same ideas.

This also gives your staff the chance to become teachers. When they teach, they learn more, too. It helps them sharpen their skills and reminds them of the fundamentals that create agency excellence.

Your new hires may have the talent, but now they need the training. The best way to convey how much you believe in your people is to give them the tools they need, and then set them free to crush it.

Discover the
Key to the Process

D o you think onboarding is an event?

Orientation is an event, and training sessions are events.

But onboarding is a process.

Events such as orientation allow new hires to learn how to use the copier and become familiar with the forms they will be using. However, a comprehensive onboarding process spans one to two years and accomplishes infinitely more. It will:

1. help you develop strong contributors.
2. convey your agency brand and values.
3. explain your culture.
4. align expectations and performance.
5. provide tools for new agents to jump right into productivity.

The only way the onboarding process can consistently produce top agents is to feed into it the right new hires. And what's the only way to ensure you've got the right agents? By using the right hiring process.

Once you implement the ten-step process, you will eliminate most of the bad candidates before they ever set foot in your office. The vast majority of prospective agents we meet never make it to the trial period; many of them don't make it past the extended interview. In our experience, a one-in-ten ratio is normal, so don't be discouraged.

No one in your organization should have to deal with the many headaches caused by frequent turnover.

Clear expectations and standards for the tryout, onboarding, and probationary periods are key. Holding them accountable from day one sets a solid tone. It allows new hires to know exactly where they stand. There are never any surprises or confusion as to what is expected of them.

If they spend their first 90 days working to reach benchmarks in order to prove themselves, then continuous high performance becomes a habit. We would all love a roster of salespeople who practice habitual excellence—and that's one of the reasons this process is so successful.

For us, there is no downside to using this hiring process. In fact, thanks to this system:

- You will be able to hire agents with no previous sales or insurance experience who will enjoy tremendous success.
- You can eliminate those frustrating hires, the people who come aboard and waste everyone's time for a short time before fizzling out.
- You can greatly reduce the amount of time and money you spend hiring and training.
- Your entire team will experience a strong sense of cohesion.

Learning to hire, manage, and coach people is no easy task. Make no mistake, this is hard work—but our business is hard. If you're attempting to run an agency on the easy road, this is not the business for you.

But if you're willing to put in the time and effort to improve yourself, your existing staff, and the hiring process, the hard work will pay off many times over.

Instead of having to make seven, eight, or even ten new hires per year just to find one agent who sticks, you can hire right the first time.

Are you going to spend more time on the front end of the hiring process than ever before? Yes—and that's where all your time *should* be spent. It's time to shift the paradigm in insurance recruitment and place the emphasis on what happens *before*, not *after* new agents are hired.

BACK TO BASICS

This hiring system will save you from some of the most painful lessons in this business. There was a point in all of our careers when we almost lost our agencies because of bad hires. The wrong team members bring with them wrong habits and attitudes, which can quickly poison the "attitude well" in your agency.

We learned the hard way. Luckily, we discovered our mistakes and realized something that all agency owners and managers need to know:

> **You can't expect staff members to habitually train and grow if you don't do the same thing. To be an effective leader, you must first lead by example.**

Successful leaders *become* their business. You and your role as agency leader are forever entwined in the same way that Tiger Woods is a "golfer" and Serena Williams is a "tennis player." When you think of Tiger, you think of golf. When you think of Serena, you think of tennis.

When people think of you, what comes to mind?

If you want to attract the right people to your agency, your *personal* brand must represent passion, excellence, and strong leadership.

Most people are not passionate about what they do for a living. Be different by being passionate about what you do, and the best candidates will naturally be attracted to your agency.

If you are always hiring, you will never feel the stress of not having enough agents to support your growth goals. Even better, bad hires will never be able to hold you prisoner or make you think you have no option but to endure them and their mediocrity.

The most important part of the following practices is that they must happen *consistently*:

Always be recruiting.

Always have a bench of redshirts.

Always be training.

Always hold your staff accountable.

Always maintain a great attitude in the agency.

Always get rid of bad apples.

And remember, anything you expect of your staff, you should expect from yourself.

Learn the One Rule
for Firing Staff

S ince we've spent so much time on hiring, it makes sense to balance it out by briefly discussing how to terminate staff.

When you use our ten-step hiring process, your terminations should be few and far between. But no matter how careful you are in your hiring, you will still need to fire someone from time to time.

First of all, don't drag your feet. Bad seeds can take root in the workplace and produce bad fruit if not pruned quickly. Gardens need to be continually tended, otherwise the weeds sap vital nutrients from the plants that are producing good fruit.

Irritating behaviors, negative attitudes, and the minimal efforts of unproductive employees can affect your agency workplace in the same way. Here are two ways to ensure that every plant in your office garden produces good fruit:

- **Be Upfront.** Regularly engage in straightforward conversations with your employees about attitudes and behavior. Don't be afraid to point out when an employee is behaving poorly or displaying an improper attitude. This will prevent frustrations from taking root.
- **Act Quickly.** Address a problem in the very moment you detect an employee doing something that bothers you or other employees. This keeps you from stewing over the situation or allowing it to stifle your own effectiveness. It also prevents a later outburst after you've allowed the problem to fester.

Minor behavioral issues are one thing; sometimes all it takes to improve a bad attitude is to clarify expectations and provide encouragement. Sometimes, that is not enough. Some issues are simply too great to overcome. How do you really know when the time is right to terminate someone? It's pretty simple. Here is the rule:

Let people go the moment you feel they are regularly taking more than they are giving.

When you run your own business, you can't afford to have an employee who is not giving 100 percent every day.

Making swift and decisive terminations will require you to make logic-based conclusions rather than react emotionally. One common problem is that we often decide to keep a problem employee based on *emotion*. Perhaps you genuinely like someone, and you don't want to fire him. You were rooting for him, but he hasn't lived up to his potential. Or you may just want to avoid confrontation.

This can make you *feel* many things, none of which help when it comes to making firm decisions about firing someone.

Acting fast—at the moment you detect the balance has shifted and someone is taking more than he or she is giving—removes the emotion and provides you with an easily recognizable termination point.

The connections we've built often cause us to hesitate. We want to give people "just one more chance." It's tempting, but giving agents too many chances means taking chances with your business.

Can you really afford that?

How often have you seen someone make a significant and positive change in productivity when you gave that person a second chance?

How often has a non-performer quickly become a star performer?

How many times has the agent who scrambles out the door at one second after 5:30 become the guy who cares so much about the client that he'll stay until the job is done?

How many negative, pessimistic employees suddenly become cheerleaders for your organization?

In our many years of experience as managers and agents, we can't think of one employee who has made a change significant enough to be worth keeping after being given "just one more chance."

The odds are against you finding the exception to this rule, and your business will suffer if you hesitate. Rid your organization of those who don't contribute to its success and guard your business against the effects of negative influences.

To assess the worth of employees who bring both positive and negative traits to the office, you have to decide if their positives outweigh their negatives. To do that, ask yourself the right questions and be honest about the answers. Here are three questions:

1. **How do I handle productive employees who have challenging attitudes?** The tougher question behind this is—why do they feel they can get away with poor behavior or lack of respect for their leaders? The answer is that *you have allowed them to*

get away with it. Employees, like students with a teacher or children with their parents, are always pushing the boundaries to see what's acceptable. When you allow your boundaries to bend, even once, it's difficult to get them back in line.

2. **Why do I continue to let them get away with such poor behavior?** The answer is you compromise your standards because you're afraid of losing their production. Don't let the fear of what *might* happen prevent you from handling a situation that *is* happening.

Employees will have greater respect for a leader who confidently and consistently maintains high standards. Make fair rules, then stand up for yourself and your business by ensuring all employees follow them.

If it becomes necessary to have a tough conversation about unacceptable behavior, you may be pleasantly surprised by how a team member responds. On the other hand, if the response is overwhelmingly negative or defensive, that person will be better off working for someone else.

3. **Do I want to lose money or make money from my hiring process?** Employees are valuable—and they can also be incredibly expensive when you hire the wrong ones! The true cost of a bad hire depends on many variables, as we discussed in the beginning of this section, and in many cases, one bad hiring decision could cost you upwards of $50,000.

Just like hiring, firing works better when you have a process in place. Take guesswork and emotion out of terminations by asking yourself the questions in this chapter and being honest in your answers.

Hiring the right people and knowing which employees to keep allows your business not only to grow but also to thrive and accelerate to new heights. With the right team in place, the potential for growth is limitless! Now get ready to talk about the next part of the H.E.R.O. system, which is your agency's environment.

E

ENVIRONMENT

Uncover the
Agency Game Changer

*I*magine walking into a large room filled with gray office furniture,
filing cabinets overflowing with stuffed manila folders, and cubicles
lining bare, windowless walls. A group of faceless employees sit in cubicles, their backs to the rest of the team. At the morning meeting, the
manager highlights who hit and who missed their numbers last week
before ending with a speech about why there can be "no more mistakes"
this quarter. After a few pats on the back, he feels he has sufficiently
motivated everyone to go out and sell.

Would you feel inspired to do your best in such an office? Would
anyone?

*Now picture yourself walking into a foyer filled with plants, mod-
ern art, and plush office furniture. Motivational quotes line the walls.
Sunlight shines on the open work space where sharply dressed professionals are on the phone. The morning meeting in the conference room is
filled with dialogue rather than a monologue, as team members role-play*

important client conversations they'll soon be having. The leader makes sure everyone has defined goals and a plan for the day, and they are sent off with sincere and positive encouragement.

In which office would you rather work?

Do you think other top performers would feel the same way?

It is your responsibility to foster an environment that people are excited to walk into every day. *Agency environment* refers to both the tangible and intangible aspects of your office—and building a positive one is a critical step in the path to accelerated growth.

On the most fundamental level, the environment represents the space around you. If your employees work in a beautiful office that they're proud to show their clients, friends, and family, you will attract first-class people who will do first-class work.

This surface level aspect of agency environment is your office image; it's the first ingredient in creating your office brand. What do people see when they walk into your office? What do you want them to think of your office and your staff?

A big part of that impression takes place before they ever visit your office or meet you face to face. Your website, social media profiles (both business and personal), blogs, and anything else you publish online or in print represents your brand. Each communication paints in your clients and prospective clients' minds a picture of what type of professional you are.

Are you a Trusted Advisor or just another insurance agent? Your online and community presence will largely determine the answer. That's why we recommend using a service such as Agency Marketing Machine (AMM), a marketer that provides comprehensive and completely "done for you" programs that are implemented systematically and consistently (more on AMM in the next chapter).

Here's why taking control of your agency brand and managing it is so important:

Whether or not you are where you want to be today from a revenue standpoint doesn't matter. What matters is that you *convey* to prospects and clients that you are successful.

You are the second most important professional in your clients' lives. Do you think your clients would enjoy showing up for a doctor's appointment only to see their doctor wearing shorts and a T-shirt and doing his exams on a card table? Of course not. Your clients want to see and feel that you've made it—whether you have or not.

Notice the word "feel." The office brand is more than just what you see. It's also what you feel.

Your environment is comprised of the way employees, clients, or anyone else *feels* when they interact with your agency. The right environment can help you reach your goals and accelerate your growth.

One aspect of the best environment that contributes more to the feel of your office than anything else is creating a culture where winning can organically take place.

> ### ASA TIP
>
> The agency culture you create should be one where everyone expects to win. Winners want to be on a team that demands excellence and consistency.

Can you imagine what it must feel like in the locker room of the team with the lead at half time of the Super Bowl? It must be positively electric. They have momentum; they ooze enthusiasm; they can sense that victory is within their reach.

It *is* possible to create that World Championship-type environment, and that is what this section—and this book and our live events and coaching—is all about.

Strive to create a culture that people are excited to work within each and every day. Your team is motivated to work within that environment, and your customers feel good when they experience your culture in action.

So, how do winners think? They know:

- If they aren't the best, that means someone else is.
- There is no value in telling others only what they *want* to hear.
- Winners do what other people are too lazy or too afraid to do. If everyone's doing it, run the other way.
- Clients don't value static content and numbers; they value real, innovative solutions that make a tangible difference in their lives.
- Complacency is an agency killer. It's never good to become satisfied with your accomplishments or to think, "I've made it."

Winners know that success is a marathon, not a sprint. Doing the right activity and having the right mindset only *some* of the time will lead to failure *every* time.

To have any chance of fostering this mindset among your team members, you have to have the right team. That is why creating the right environment has a lot to do with hiring the right people. Once you have the right people, they must be properly trained, which is a lengthy process that includes instilling in them a set of expectations.

Once they understand your expectations, crafting the right environment means following up on those expectations, or as we like to say, *inspecting what you expect.* If you don't inspect what you expect, there is only one person at fault for a lack of results.

Have you ever stopped and thought about how your office feels when new candidates or customers walk through your door?

If you had to rate your office "feel" on a scale from one to ten, where would it be right now?

If you're like us, that question wasn't a top priority when you started your agency. The most important question was something like, "How can I make the most money and find good agents to work for me?"

Here's the secret: One of the most overlooked answers to that question we all have as agency owners is by creating the right environment!

Do you want clients to interact with your company in a way that goes beyond simple transactional selling? Do you want people to *love* doing business with you?

What will make them feel that way? It's your brand—which includes the physical and mental environment you surround yourself with, foster, and encourage among employees.

It's also critical to create a Trusted Advisor agency, which is the focus of the next chapter. At the end of the book, the bonus chapter will highlight the winning traits that every Trusted Advisor has in common.

If you focus on doing everything you can as a Trusted Advisor for your clients *and* your staff, your business will reach new, soaring heights. Policies, politics, products, and profit—none of them will be an issue when your environment is one of positive motivation and sincere encouragement based on the personal relationships you form with your team of equals.

You can have the best processes in the world, along with the best intentions, but if your environment is undesirable and your culture is negative, in all likelihood you'll fall short of the success you're looking for, and deserve.

We've coached winning agencies and struggling agencies, and over time, we noticed a trend. When an agency is unsuccessful, there are some telltale signs we notice right away within the culture. The same goes for the high-performing ones. Successful agencies *always* display these critical actions, which will be the focus of our section on environment. Winning agencies:

1. Create a "Trusted Advisor" agency.
2. Let go of the pursuit of perfection.
3. Work toward a common goal.
4. Make attitude a conscious choice.
5. Lead by example.
6. Treat employees like family.

There are no magic formulas, secret steps, or silver bullets for instant agency success. But if we were to pick *the* biggest factor in changing our offices from money-bleeders to money-feeders, it would be the environment.

Creating an environment that inspires your staff and elicits trust will skyrocket you to success faster and more effectively than virtually anything else in your business. Simple adjustments to your agency's physical and psychological environment can make sweeping changes to the type of people you attract and the level of success you achieve.

Create a Trusted
Advisor Culture

Trusted Advisor [noun]:
An insurance expert and "people person" who values
maintaining a relationship more than the outcome of
any particular transaction.

One of the fundamentals of any good environment is to find your focus.

But where should that focus be? Is it really just a "numbers game" like we so often hear in this industry?

While we agree that numbers are a critical piece of the puzzle, overemphasizing that perspective can be damaging. In the quest to increase your bottom line and create a thriving, successful business, it is what those numbers represent—i.e., your customers—that are the key.

That's why in our agencies, we strive to create more than just a sales environment. Yes, "sales" is what we do. But a customer is not a number or a sale.

A customer is a relationship, and within that relationship, we serve as the second most important professional in that customer's life.

We are Trusted Advisors. We come from agencies that stand out amidst a sea of other agencies. A Trusted Advisor places more value on maintaining and preserving the relationship itself than on the outcome of any particular transaction.

Most of us are only focused on activity, ideas, and transactions, but if you shift into the role of Trusted Advisor, people will *want* to do business with you. Here are the three main operating principles of a Trusted Advisor:

1. Continually focus on the customer rather than themselves.
2. Habitually find new ways to be of greater service to others.
3. Always do the right thing regardless of whether it increases the bottom line.

It can be challenging to focus on doing the right thing over the outcome when your pay is driven by outcome—but doing what's right will pave the way to long-term success and career satisfaction.

Creating a dynamic environment and an advisor-based culture is all about finding ways to build real relationships with clients. The best way to do that is to build relationships through emotion rather than logic.

Logic leads to price—and nowhere else.

Logic says, "Let's match every line of these two competing policies using an apples-to-apples comparison. We'll get it exactly the same and compare to find out which number at the bottom is lower."

Never, and we mean *never*, do an apples-to-apples comparison. That is what transactional agencies do.

Trusted Advisors take extra time to tailor each policy to the customer's needs.

When you come from a place of emotion, you invite all the senses to the party. The sales interaction then becomes much more than a product presentation. You are effectively selling customers on the idea of doing business with *you*, regardless of who else offers to shave a few dollars off their monthly premium.

In this industry, there is always going to be another agency offering products similar to yours. So how do you stand out? By being different!

What sets you apart? A more important question: do you even know what sets you apart?

If you are unsure, start by asking some of your loyal customers what comes to mind when they think of your agency. You may hear things like "fast customer service" or "friendly faces" or "trusted expert advice." Whatever it is, you can begin to use those as the basis for differentiating yourself.

If you don't like what you hear, that's another matter entirely.

When you can successfully convey to customers what differentiates you from the competition, the value of doing business with you begins to outweigh boring, black-and-white, insignificant price considerations—and that's when people are moved to make a decision.

Make it all about the customer. In a world where nobody listens, be the exception.

Don't sell them; be their Trusted Advisor.

LISTEN YOUR WAY TO MORE SALES

People want to do business with people they know, like, and trust. That means it's your job to train your staff on how to have the kinds of conversations that enable clients to know, like, and trust them.

For example, people love to talk about themselves, which is why we train our teams to ask questions and let prospects do the talking—we call it "listening your way into a sale." A customer may not remember everything you said, but he will remember a good listener over someone who tried to talk his or her way into a sale.

When you sell through emotion, you seek to find out about clients and their needs. Rushing through a sales presentation may mean you can call on more prospects that day, but it certainly doesn't convey the fact that you care. So, if you really *do* care, one of the fundamentals is to spend as much time as necessary developing relationships.

We believe our clients are serving their best interests by coming to our agencies. In instances where this is not the case (and it does happen), we let them know that it might be best to stay where they are. But any time we ask them to purchase a policy through us, we know they are making the right decision.

If you have a similar conviction about your agency, that doesn't always mean clients will save money. There are times when a customer might pay *more* money to work with you.

You can feel comfortable, even confident, asking them to do this—once you show them the true value (not just the price) of your products and exceptional client service.

We supply our staff with a list of the reasons people should choose our agencies, and we encourage them to internalize these reasons. Your environment feeds off your value to customers, which means you must effectively convey the advantages of doing business with you that have nothing to do with products or price.

Aren't customers just looking for the lowest price? Some are. But in our experience, most people will forego that priority to do business with a person who genuinely cares about them, listens to them, and delivers exceptional service. Those customers will become your most loyal ones, the ones who help you create a top agency.

We want our employees to talk about anything *other* than selling insurance when they engage with brand new prospects. That is the time to get to know them, because the bottom line is:

This is not the insurance business; it's the people business.

BUILD A MARKETING MACHINE

If you want to create a Trusted Advisor environment, you must expertly mold public perception of you and your agency. Before you can impress a client with how well you are dressed or how sharp your agency looks, you must put out into the world what you and your agency represent. Consider the following aspects of your agency brand:

- **Digital presence.** Your prospects and customers are online searching, clicking, and being social. Are you engaging them?
- **Community involvement.** Giving back matters to your customers. What are you doing to show that your agency is different from the rest and gives back?
- **Public relations.** Is your agency being positively or negatively promoted in the media? Is it being promoted at all?
- **Brand identity.** Are you recognized by prospects? For what?
- **Newsletters, emails, and texts.** How are you connecting regularly to stay top of mind with your client base?

Managing so many moving parts to your brand is hard. We use Agency Marketing Machine (AMM), a tool that helps agency owners with all of these elements so you can focus on excelling and doing what you do best.

AMM uses a wide variety of methods to strengthen agency relationships with current clients, gain new clients, and become a highly trusted and admired partner in your agency's community. To learn more, visit: agencymarketingmachine.com.

Whether you use a marketing service or not, those elements of your brand must be a primary focus. So, define your brand. Then, build a marketing machine within your agency to promote it!

CREATE A RECOMMENDATION-BASED CULTURE

If you believe you are in the people business, then the next part of creating the right culture should be a no-brainer for you.

Ask for recommendations.

You may know them as "referrals," but we like to call them recommendations since that is a word people are used to seeing and using on social media.

There is no greater way to grow your agency than by creating a book of business filled with customers who are partnering with you because of a referral or recommendation from someone else.

If you and your staff don't get more referrals, the primary reasons may be because you:

- Don't remember to ask.
- Don't know how to ask effectively.
- Feel you have already taken too much of people's time.
- Feel like you already sold them something.
- Feel you don't deserve it or are too embarrassed.

- Didn't get good results in the past.
- Don't feel that asking for referrals provides a big enough incentive for customers.

If you've done a great job and treated a customer like an individual and not a number, you should feel honored to ask for recommendations. If you believe you don't deserve one, then you are not giving great service.

Build a recommendation-based culture within your agency. It's a lot less expensive than other advertising methods, promotes retention, and is far more time efficient. Approach your interactions as a Trusted Advisor, and you will never feel too intimidated to ask for recommendations.

NETWORKING BREEDS RELATIONSHIPS

Modern prospecting is becoming less about traditional cold calling and more about who you know and how you connect with them. In fact, thanks to the advent of networking groups, the massive amount of information available online, and the prevalence of social media, there is really no reason to make a purely "cold" call anymore, especially with no prior knowledge about the person you're calling.

We have tried every possible way to prospect for new customers, and we have found time and time again that the most positive agency environment is formed on networking—and specifically, on seeking out referral sources.

The right networking mix can provide you with constant, solid leads. That helps prevent your agents from feeling the stinging frustration of calling an endless list of prospects who have no connection with anyone or anything in your business.

For us, mortgage referrals are a major key to our success, which is why we encourage our agents to go out and find as many mortgage referral sources as they can.

When our agents receive referrals from their mortgage sources, they act quickly and provide instant feedback to the source on the outcome of the connection. They make sure to convey their appreciation and their desire to help the referral source in any way they can.

The best networking is always a two-way street.

Another effective way to foster a networking environment is to ask customers to recommend you to others. For our agents, this ask has become a part of every sale. At the conclusion of a successful close, our agents let clients know that they value and respect their clients' input and would love their advice on who might also want to benefit by becoming a client.

Our agents then put pen to paper—writing their new client's name at the top and numbering it down the side—and then hand it to their client, with the expectation that he or she will write down some names.

That type of physical action is key to gaining more qualified referrals and nurturing your networking environment.

THE METHOD BEHIND THE MADNESS

How do we train our staff and foster this relationship-centered environment where the customer is first, employees are equals, networking is encouraged, and everyone is working toward a common goal?

We use a lot of the same things you do: We have new recruits shadow seasoned recruits; we listen to their phone calls and provide positive coaching; and we go with them into the field to show them how to run a meeting with a client.

But there is one thing that sets our training apart from average agencies, and it goes back to something from our childhood. When we were kids, there was one reason our parents could always give that was incapable of being debated:

"Because I said so."

Somewhere along the way in our teens, that reason no longer sufficed, did it? We eventually demanded to know the *why* behind what we were being asked to do.

Despite the fact that "because I said so" loses its power as we get older, we've all witnessed, worked for, or even been the kinds of leaders who expect their teams to do something without being told why.

If you want to run a successful agency, "because I said so" is simply not good enough.

You cannot lead team members in this manner; it's condescending. They deserve to know the why behind what they are being told to do.

Bosses bark orders and fire people.

Leaders give the why behind the logical steps they are proposing.

Once you step outside the stereotypical role of *boss*—someone who gives commands with no explanation—it opens up a whole new world in the area of training. In fact, it can take the very idea of "training" and turn it into a dynamic, fluid experience that becomes enjoyable and encouraging, rather than frustrating and intimidating.

We used to lead by telling, not teaching. After a while, we were forced to take a look in the mirror and notice the one common denominator present when morale was low and agents were underproducing.

Fancy training manuals and online skills courses don't create winners. That's *your* job—and you do that by getting down on the level of your employees and explaining the why behind what you are teaching.

We were able to change our leadership and coaching styles by doing exactly what you are doing right now. We found mentors who had "been there, done that." Where did we find them? We read their books!

Years ago, it became our goal to train staff to provide the highest quality service and to maintain that outstanding customer service. Our agencies now run on the highest quality training in the industry.

Once our agents are licensed, we consider it our responsibility to train them for success. That is a responsibility embedded within our environments.

And when you think about it, why wouldn't you do this? If you invest all the time, money, and effort it takes to hire top agents, it just makes sense to provide them with the best possible opportunity to succeed after you bring them on board.

We believe the best way to engrain best practices is to *show* rather than *tell*. Our new hires spend a lot of time with us in the beginning— the agency owners and not just a manager or top agent—so they can see exactly how we want them to work each lead, from front to back.

Contrast that to when we first started. We threw new agents into the deep end and figured the good ones would swim. Then we wondered why we were left with mediocre performers and high turnover.

How could we expect new hires to do it "the right way" without showing them what that entailed?

Listening in on calls is invaluable, which is why our agencies heavily utilize phone systems in training. When new hires are on the phone with clients, the leadership can monitor them and even whisper some helpful advice during the call. Conversely, the new hires can listen in on top agents' client calls to see how the pros do it.

Directly after the call, everyone can discuss the process (including the whys behind what makes it work).

Since the phone is the agency's lifeline, we make it a goal to get new hires to fail on the phone 1,000 times within three months. "Failure" doesn't exactly sound positive, but for new hires, it's necessary.

By acknowledging it up front and even making failure a goal, it takes away much of the fear that comes with phone prospecting. By failing 1,000 times, it allows new hires to cram one year's worth of failure into 90 days.

If that sounds intimidating, it can be. But it also has a *huge* upside— it will greatly speed up the learning process and build confidence and resilience when new agents need it most.

A good phone system is key, as are other technology tools. Any tool you can provide to your employees that makes their job easier is worth it. Outdated technology creates unnecessary roadblocks that can be easily avoided.

You must ensure you provide the best office in the business, with great benefits, mutual respect, frequent recognition, and modern conveniences. An investment on the front end will save you money down the road in hiring and training costs because turnover will be lower.

What type of training do you currently utilize? Is it working well for your employees? Do you give the why behind what you teach?

If you are taking your time in the hiring process and being selective and yet still experiencing frequent turnover and average results, it is possible you are not giving employees what they really need.

A good coach explains the method behind the madness.

KEEP YOUR EYE ON THE PRIZE

Conducting your training in this manner will only lead to good outcomes. Employees will more easily remember what you teach when they know the reasons behind it. They will feel more confident in performing actions since they know why those actions are so vital. Most importantly, they will have a set of expectations that lead to the results both they *and* you want.

Results are as important as expectations, but they can only be achieved consistently if you manage the activities that *lead* to those results. Managing activities does not mean sending out warning emails near the end of the quarter stating that certain goals or quotas have not yet been met.

Goals are only as helpful as we allow them to be. According to Mark McCormack, author of *What They Don't Teach You at Harvard Business School*, interviewers surveyed new graduates from Harvard's MBA Program in 1979 and found that:

- 84 percent had no specific goals at all.
- 13 percent had goals, but they were not committed to paper.
- 3 percent had clear, written goals and plans to accomplish them.

In 1989, the graduates were interviewed again, revealing some shocking (or maybe not so shocking) results:

- The 13 percent of the class who had goals were earning, on average, twice as much as the 84 percent who had no goals at all.
- The 3 percent who had clear, written goals were earning, on average, ten times as much as the other 97 percent put together.

Goals help us believe in ourselves. They tell us what we truly want. They also hold us accountable for our failures—but none of that is true if you don't keep those goals at the forefront of your mind through daily reminders.

There is no excuse for a producer to progress through the month blindly and wake up at the end and say, "Well, I didn't hit my goal." Specific, definable, and measurable actions must be taken in order to get there. Do your employees know what those actions are and why they will allow them to reach their goals?

They need to know exactly what it takes. How many telemarketing hours should they be putting in? How much premium per day should they be writing to stay on track? How many phone calls should they each be making on a daily basis?

ASA TIP

Sit down with your team every week and have them write down their weekly goals, both personal and business. This will help everyone remain consistently focused.

It's this level of follow-through that will help create an efficient and productive working environment for your staff.

Shape Your
Agency's Attitude

When you wake up in the morning, do you know what determines how your day will go? We'll give you a hint: it has absolutely nothing to do with anything that happens *to* you or *around* you.

Your attitude alone can determine what type of day, week, month, year, and life you will have. That may seem oversimplified, but it's not.

It's not easy, but it really is that straightforward.

As a leader, the attitude you choose when you wake up in the morning will set the tone for the entire office. If you're not creating the right environment within yourself, instead choosing to carry the weight of the world on your shoulders, how can you expect your staff to fight past rejection without feeling deflated?

It is your attitude that allows you to display one of the biggest game changers in agency growth—and that is consistency.

Be consistent. That is another thing that is simple but not always easy. Yes, life is complicated and messy. But when you step into your agency, those messy things don't matter. What matters is that you do the same activity every day and expect the same from your staff.

You could equate it to watching NBA and WNBA players on the basketball court. Those athletes undoubtedly have plenty of things going on in their lives, but when they enter that arena, it's show time. Similarly, you have to put your best foot forward when you enter your arena.

When you come in smiling (even when you don't feel like it), people around you are going to smile. That's actually a scientifically proven phenomenon. According to recent studies, we automatically mimic the smiles or frowns of others because it helps our brains better understand what other people are feeling, and this allows us to respond appropriately.[2]

Even better, when we mimic someone else's facial expression, we trigger that same emotional state in ourselves, which then allows us to formulate an appropriate social response.

So a smile—and the positive attitude that comes with it—is truly contagious!

If you have things going on at home, leave them at home. You can focus on improving your home life away from work, but you must compartmentalize the emotions that come with the ups and downs of both family and work life.

In short, never allow either environment to poison the other one.

PROMOTE PURE POSITIVITY

Attitude is arguably *the* most critical determinant of your agency environment. Our agency environments thrive on pure positivity. Our

---

2 Wood, Adrienne et al. "Fashioning the Face: Sensorimotor Simulation Contributes to Facial Expression Recognition." *Trends in Cognitive Sciences*, Volume 20, Issue 3, pp. 227–240.

goal is to create environments that are constantly upbeat, motivating, and encouraging. That is the type of energy that fuels an agency and keeps propelling it forward.

On any given day at our offices, you will hear music playing and find inspirational quotes waiting for you in your inbox. These little things become some of the biggest influencers in a positive office environment.

Why is attitude so paramount to your success? Because people ultimately have no control over their intrinsic ability or talent, but they *certainly* have control over their efforts and their attitude.

If your agency is a place where attitudes are positive and optimistic, where your employees know that you care and that you're trying to do the right thing for the agency, for them, and for customers, you will find that you have to work to motivate a lot less.

That's because real motivation comes from within. It comes from knowing someone has your back; it comes from surrounding yourself with positivity and can-do attitudes; it comes from feeling appreciated.

We encourage that level of motivation on a daily basis through the environments we have created. Whenever someone closes a sale, everyone in the office knows about it and cheers. This is a great way to keep the fire lit under employees all day long. Creating an email chain to congratulate an agent on new business can also work because recognition drives momentum.

You can provide tangible rewards for closing sales. Examples include being able to play a little mini basketball, putt golf balls, or take a turn in the "closer's massage chair" in the break room. Your team should truly enjoy their time at work. Their job is not easy, and you will notice a huge improvement in attitude when your team members get to break up the day with short bursts of fun.

REWARD POSITIVE RESULTS

If recognition drives momentum, then rewards are like the fuel that can turn a campfire of momentum into a blazing inferno of activity and results.

People love rewards and incentives, and we use that fact to propel our teams forward and keep attitudes high. We want our staff to feel appreciated for their hard work, so we offer trips, spa days, and other prizes for reaching certain goals.

Getting a nice paycheck is not enough; rewards must be personal, and they must also be directly targeted at what specifically motivates your team.

It's also a good idea to make a big deal about birthdays. Just because we aren't kids anymore doesn't mean birthdays can't be fun. Most of us still love when people make a little bit of a fuss on our big day.

It's wise to ask employees whether they actually want to have their birthday acknowledged (there may be a few people who would prefer a quiet acknowledgement or no celebration at all).

Only celebrate birthdays if you are going to be consistent—it's everyone or no one. Celebrating some birthdays while forgetting others will have the opposite effect of what you intended.

And don't forget about Christmas! The holiday season is a great time to foster a good environment. If you're not paying Christmas bonuses, you should. We let our staff know that if their performance remains solid throughout the year, the Christmas bonuses are going to be solid—and the Christmas parties will be epic.

Earlier we mentioned that a nice paycheck is not enough. While that may be true, it is also the most important "reward" your employees receive. That is why it's critical to ensure your team knows exactly how they get paid.

Every month, we sit down with our staff to uncover any missed income opportunities. Then we discuss what they can do next month to make sure they don't leave that same money on the table.

The hope is that they will eventually understand the pay system so well that they can come to us and show us what they left on the table. If they have a crystal-clear understanding of how they get paid, it will motivate them to step it up.

If it doesn't, that tells you everything you need to know about them.

ENCOURAGE HEALTHY COMPETITION

Results are great—and they are even more valuable when they are compared to the results of others.

Healthy competition is a key motivator in a positive agency environment.

This starts with clear expectations. For example, our producers know that they are each expected to write a certain amount in premium per month (typically $25,000). By setting that expectation, everybody knows where the bar is set and what needs to happen in order to reach it.

We also don't want agents to settle for the minimum; we want them to reach higher. To encourage that that kind of effort, you could set up a series of levels, or clubs, ranging in $10,000 increments up to $80,000. By being a member of a certain club, it means an agent has written at least that amount of premium in one month.

Your best salespeople are driven by competition, and if they find themselves in one of the lower tiers for a few months, it will motivate them to fight harder the next month.

You may also choose to send a motivational email every morning. In that email, you can include the standings, which is a running tally of every item that each salesperson has written for the week, including total premium, number of referrals, and other important figures.

Healthy competition is a great motivator for driven salespeople. Ambitious employees want to see their names at the top of the list. The best of the best are ultra-competitive, so show them the scoreboard. Let them know who's winning and who's climbing the ranks, because that will drive them to a whole new level.

DRESS FOR THE ATTITUDE YOU WANT

Think about when you see someone who is impeccably dressed and groomed. The first question that comes to mind is, "Wow, what do they do for a living? That person must have an important role in a successful company."

Your attire and grooming can play a major role in the ease with which new customers learn to trust you and believe what you are saying. Since we are the second most important professionals in our clients' lives, it is our responsibility to look the part.

> ### ASA TIP
>
> Our motto is "dress to impress." For a lot of our agents, that means wearing a suit every day. Decide what "dress to impress" means to your agency and expect your staff to look the part.

It's not only clients who are affected by our choice of attire. According to *The Wall Street Journal*, recent studies suggest that wearing nice clothing such as a suit or a blazer "may raise one's confidence level, affect how others perceive the wearer, and in some cases, even boost the level of one's abstract thinking, the type in which leaders and executives engage."[3]

---

3 http://www.wsj.com/articles/why-dressing-for-success-leads-to-success-1456110340

When we tried casual Fridays, we noticed that "casual Friday" quickly became "casual workday." Do you think clients expect you to look and act your best only from Monday through Thursday?

You must ensure that the office environment is unchanged from day to day, which means that Hawaiian Shirt Day might need to be replaced with another incentive. People and clients will respect you for dressing for success.

UNCOVER ATTITUDE ASSASSINS

In Chapter 10, we talked about how misplaced emotions are often a silent saboteur of a positive environment. There is another sneaky culprit ready to undo all of your hard work—an attitude assassin.

Attitude assassins are people who breed discontent, cause problems for customers, colleagues and managers, and/or lack ethics. These employees can cause irreparable damage in your office.

The problem is, these employees are not always bad at their jobs. It could be an employee who is great at her job but speaks to customers with utter contempt. It might be a stellar salesperson who is a top producer but treats support staff like lowly peasants. Maybe it is an employee who says all the right things to you but then turns around and bad-mouths the agency to other employees and customers.

Left untended, that individual can create problems with customers and other employees, spoil the agency environment, and severely damage your agency's reputation.

In the iconic book *Good to Great*, author Jim Collins researched 1,400+ companies and discovered a set of ideas that, when embraced and implemented, set "great" companies apart from "good" ones. One of Collins' discoveries was that businesses with toxic employees usually had an environment or a culture that enabled them to be so.

In short, any agency that allows poison pills to remain is communicating a tolerance for mediocrity that will keep it from greatness.

The best way to avoid a toxic employee is through a stringent screening and hiring process. However, there will be times when an attitude assassin slips through the cracks and ends up in your agency.

When this happens, document the issue *properly,* and deal with it *promptly.* If the poisonous attitude cannot be eradicated, that employee would be better off working somewhere else.

It's unrealistic to believe that your employees are not going to ever be negative, engage in water cooler talk from time to time, or occasionally discuss things they don't like about the agency. We tell new employees they will inevitably encounter some negativity in the office, but when they need to be reminded of why they are working there, they can consciously choose to shift their focus to what makes the agency great.

No environment is ever perfect, but if you openly communicate and quickly provide solutions for eradicating poisonous attitudes, you can make it the best office it can be.

HAVE A LITTLE FUN

What we do is important, but let's be honest—no one ever grew up dreaming of being an insurance agent. There are times when the tasks we do are boring and repetitive. We don't work for a hip tech company. We don't drive racecars. We sell insurance, but that doesn't mean we can't shake things up from time to time and have a fun office.

There is virtually no end to the kinds of games you can play in the office that make things more interesting and add some variety to the week.

For example, you can play "Wheel of Fortune," where employees win spins on the wheel by hitting certain office-wide goals. You can put gift cards, rounds of golf, or even weekend getaways on the wheel as prizes.

You can even set up a game where each week team members submit their best example of a time when they turned a problem into an opportunity. Each submission is presented to the office, and the best one is chosen. The winner receives some universally desirable reward such as a gift card, gas card, or cash.

Making things fun is never a bad idea—in fact, when you make the office a fun place to work, you will reap the benefits in more ways than you could imagine. Improved attitudes and heightened morale are obvious outcomes. But you will also see greater productivity.

As a bonus, you will also naturally attract more positive candidates who want to work in a positive, upbeat environment. We may not be working for Google or Facebook, but who says insurance can't be fun?

Expect to Win

Because this book is about taking your agency to the next level and beyond, we are going to continue our discussion of attitude in a different, more advanced, and even more impactful way.

We love to use professional athletes and their training and preparation strategies as a benchmark for whether we are engaging in the kinds of activities and adopting the kinds of attitudes that lead to success. Why?

Because they are the best in the world—and that is exactly how we want to be able to describe our own businesses.

Visualization has long been an integral part of professional sports. Imagining yourself besting the competition has proven so effective that sports psychologists (like the ones who work with Olympians) say that more than ever, the way to victory is to put yourself in the contest mentally and visualize winning the gold.

These days, athletes are taking this visualization a step further. "Visualization, for me, doesn't take in all the senses," said Emily Cook, a U.S. freestyle aerial skiing Olympian. "You have to smell it. You have to hear it. You have to feel it—everything."

Insurance salespeople may not be able to mentally put themselves into a physical contest of strength and agility where they work to overcome the competition. But that's because, for most of us, our biggest obstacles to overcome are the conceptual limits we set for ourselves.

Not sure you'll write a policy today? *You probably won't.*

Don't think you'll win the trip this quarter for hitting your numbers? *You are absolutely right.*

The mental battle in which we engage on a daily basis is not easily won. If it were, everybody would be in sales! Our profession isn't for the faint of heart. We are not like the desk jockeys of the world who clock in, do mindless work, and then clock out.

What we do is hard! But that's also why the potential payoff is so great.

"Expect to Win" is a sales philosophy, but also so much more. We have found that human beings tend to live up or down to the expectations we set for ourselves. And if you ask, most people will tell you that they *do* expect to win… sometimes. They also expect that other times, they won't lose too badly.

But isn't any kind of loss still a loss? Big or small, it means you went for something and didn't get it. So, if you have in your mind that there will be times when you may not be successful, then you are doing a serious disservice to your customers, your paycheck, your career, and your agency.

When the best of the best Major League hitters step up to the plate, they don't expect to hit a double. They don't imagine themselves getting tagged out as they round third base.

They *expect* to hit a homerun!

So much of the time, we accept the fact that we may not come out on top this time around. And it's okay, right? We gotta cut ourselves some slack, right?

No, we do not!

The best *never* do.

This "Well, I don't expect to win *every* time" mentality causes unnecessary struggle in our industry. And if we're being honest, believing and living out this approach is code for, "I do just enough not to get fired and keep the bills paid."

Plenty of careers can pay the bills. Plenty will put food on your table. But if you have voluntarily chosen to engage in this career for all its potential, why not set yourself up for success?

Why not *expect to win*?

THE PROBLEM WITH WINNING

In our experience, there are two kinds of salespeople. First, there are the ones willing to show up—but that's about it. Their predominant thought is, "Man, it'd be nice if Mr. Prospect bought something today." They certainly don't assume Mr. Prospect is going to buy. They aren't going to fight for that win. Nor will they lose sleep if he doesn't.

Then, there are the few salespeople who expect to win. And not just sometimes—*every* time. Their overriding thought is, "Mrs. Prospect needs what I have to offer, and I want to be the one to help her."

In our experience, their closing ratio is two to three times higher than everyone else's.

The specific behaviors of salespeople reflect their mindset—and it's the behaviors of standout salespeople that lead to more sales and greater satisfaction for everyone.

The good news is that anyone can learn these winning behaviors and mindsets. And the great news is that even if you don't habitually expect to win yet, you already know what it feels like.

Think about the times when you knew you were going to win a game. Maybe your team was ahead, and you sensed victory was imminent. The look on your face changed, your outlook became sunny and bright, and even your tone of voice became different. What's more significant is that everyone around you detected that confidence.

In short, your expectation of winning became palpable!

As a salesperson who expects to win, when you build rapport, you are doing so with the expectation that this *will* become a long-term relationship. Believe it or not, your prospect can feel this expectation and will respond accordingly.

Of course, there is a downside to setting up the expectation to win. In fact, it's the biggest reason most people in this profession do *not* expect to win every time and are ultimately not as successful as they could be.

The problem is fear—but we're not talking about the fear of losing. We are talking about the fear of *winning*.

When you succeed, everything changes because people expect you to be successful again! They expect you to do the same things over and over that made you victorious. If your kid gets all A's on her report card, don't you expect the same of her on the next report card?

What do most people do to avoid such pressure? They keep expectations low, because a lack of expectations means an easier life—at least that's the way it seems.

Not everyone is willing to work hard consistently. And since hard work and winning go hand in hand, that means those who are not willing to do the work will have careers that include a few decent wins along with a lot more losses.

That's okay! We'll let them continue to set mediocre expectations and receive the mediocre results that follow, because that equates to more victories for those of us who *expect* those victories.

This is not some Kumbaya or "life is peachy" attitude. In fact, great salespeople are not inherently optimistic; nor do they have to be. They *do* have to be willing to work hard, and more importantly, to practice believing and living out the expectation that they *will* win. It's not even a matter of *if*. It's just a matter of *when*.

HOW TO IMPLEMENT THIS EXPECTATION

Is this one of those "this sounds easy, but it's not" kind of things?

Yes and no.

Making "Expect to Win" a consistent part of your mindset is a process. However, there is one principle that, once internalized, will make this mentality easier to adopt than you might realize.

> **Do you believe that what you are offering will better someone else's life? If you don't, you need to—because *that* is the key.**

It has to be about them, not about you.

It has to be about their future, not about your product or service.

You win because they win!

Here are a few key ways to implement this mentality successfully into your agency:

1. Drink the Kool-Aid.

As the agency leader, you must be a student of attitude. If you are not "drinking the Kool-Aid" and have not personally bought into the idea that the right attitudes and expectations are everything in this business, you should get out of the game. In order for this philosophy to infiltrate your organization, it must first fully inundate you. Only then can you translate it to them.

2. Model the behavior.

Drinking the Kool-Aid also makes it possible for you to carry out the next important step, which is to model the expectations you expect from your team. You and all of the leaders in your agency have to walk the walk and definitely not just talk the talk.

3. Say it aloud.

Another integral part of this process is to harness the power of the spoken word. *We believe whatever comes out of our mouths.* This has been proven time and time again. Speaking positive words aloud is also inspirational, which is important because commission-based selling can be a scary thing. Grow their confidence and their self-belief by speaking about winning daily, even hourly. Set the expectation to win by saying it aloud, letting your team know that you expect *them* to expect to win!

4. Look for footprints on the dance floor.

As a leader, it's your job to stay focused on improving—as an agency, as a boss, as a parent, as a friend, and more. When it comes to your team, this means you must help them focus on getting better as well. Listen for the outstanding things your agents said and did, then encourage them to repeat those winning behaviors. Chances are, they are not entirely sure exactly what led to victory. Therefore, they are less likely to repeat those winning actions; it is up to you to help them understand *why* they won.

Just as important, listen for those things that made them sound less confident. For example, after an objection like, "I'll think about it," a typical salesperson says, "Well, let me know" before hanging up and writing it off as a lost sale. Instead of ending the conversation this way, try a different approach, such as:

> "I understand that; I'm the exact same way. Mr. Prospect, why don't you jot down your questions as you think of them, and I'll answer them for you when we speak again."

When you respond to an objection in this manner, you are not just expecting to win for your own sake. You are setting up the expectation in your prospect's mind that you can *both* still win. They can also sense that you respect them and do not want to pressure them.

Remember, most people respond to sales pressure by either pushing back or giving in, but often feeling secretly resentful of strong-arm tactics. Likewise, they also view a lack of effort or follow-up questions as you not being serious about your job, which hurts your reputation as a Trusted Advisor.

The Expect-to-Win philosophy strikes a healthy balance between the two and allows space for everyone to feel victorious.

THE SECRET TO WINNING

The Baseball Hall of Fame includes just 226 major league players. Considering it has been open since 1939, that's not very many names.

Why do so few players make the cut?

The reason is that most hitters have bad habits they can't break. Some like the ball to be close. Others like it farther away. Either way, pitchers know what kind of hitter their opponent is when he steps up to the plate, and they pitch accordingly.

"You like the ball away? I'll throw it close."

"You like it close? I'll throw it away."

Since most hitters are never able to change their swing, their averages remain… pretty average throughout their careers.

But then there are the unicorns of the sport—the Hall of Famers. Where do they want the pitcher to throw the ball? Here's the thing:

It doesn't matter.

The best players think, "Throw it wherever you want. I'll hit it anywhere!"

This is exactly what the Expect-to-Win mentality instills in you! That is also why this mindset is the best way to overcome anything and everything a prospect can throw at you.

It doesn't matter what objection you hear. It Just. Doesn't. Matter.

"I want to shop around." *It doesn't matter.*

"I understand. I shop around, too. Don't just shop policies and prices. Shop me, too. Then let's reconnect after you've shopped around."

"It's not the right time." *It doesn't matter.*

"I understand. Timing is important. Let's talk about how we can help if it makes sense—and it might not right now. But we can take a look and make sure."

You shouldn't feel "lucky" when you have a win. Wins should be the natural conclusion to a productive, mutually beneficial conversation with a customer.

You should already be expecting it. And it has nothing to do with luck.

Because this is something that must be engrained, it also means that there is no off-season when it comes to teaching this philosophy to your team. It's a moment-to-moment kind of thing, and there is never a time when teaching it becomes less important.

WHAT IF I REALLY DON'T WIN?

When you expect to win, what happens if you don't? Does that mean your mental game failed you? Is there something you could have done differently? Maybe you didn't believe enough?

This is a complicated issue and causes a real fork in the road. You failed, but winners know that does not equate to failure. So, what do you do?

First, don't chalk the failure up as inevitable (even though we all experience situations that don't go the way we expected). Believing some failures to be "inevitable" robs you of the chance to learn from them. When you expect to win but don't, this should cause you to want to dig until you figure out if there was something you could have done differently.

There may not have been. You may have done everything absolutely perfectly. But chances are, that is not the case.

So, start digging. Talk to someone else for insights. Ask for outside advice. Turn to a mentor or a coach. This applies not just to your team, but to you, the leader, as well.

Being humble enough to admit you're not perfect is an integral part of this philosophy.

Sometimes you examine what went wrong and realize that the real win *was* the loss. For example, not every person can afford what you have to offer. When some people say, "I can't afford this," they really mean it!

In such cases, you win by not overextending such prospects. This goes back to the key principle behind the Expect-to-Win philosophy:

It's about them, not about you!

Of course, wins can be hard to define because "winning" looks a little different for everyone. However, there is one universal truth that applies to every single one of us:

Failure is when you perform at less than *your* best.

Your best and someone else's best are not going to be the same. A high school tennis player is not a failure because she can't serve with as much power as a Wimbledon champion. That is why the Expect-to-Win philosophy requires you not to compare yourself to anyone other than the best version of *you*.

This is almost harder than an outside comparison because many of us prefer not to self-reflect if we can avoid it. But if you are not actively and consciously working to make yourself better, then you will never attain the greatness you envision.

In fact, adopting the Expect-to-Win philosophy requires so much mental effort and introspection that it's really a *lifestyle* rather than a mindset.

For now, the most important takeaway is this—for the things that are most important to you, measure yourself against *your own best effort*.

The idea of giving your own best effort every day is overwhelming to some, but when you boil it down, it's really very simple:

You can expect to win, or you can expect not to.

Either way, you are going to be right.

Lead by
Letting Go

If someone barks at you to complete a task, you probably do it.

When someone empowers you to complete a task and allows you the space to make it your own, you likely do it as well.

If both methods get the job done, then what does it matter?

Well, let us ask you a question: Do you want people to do just enough not to get fired, or do you want a team of motivated professionals you can trust to be ambassadors of your agency brand in the world?

When people manage through fear, they can get results. When everyone knows you're "the boss," you aren't necessarily going to fail. But you certainly won't thrive.

When you operate in a way that screams, "I'm in charge," what you usually get is uninspired work. You get people who do just enough not to get fired. You get people who are living paycheck to paycheck with no purpose, inspiration, or creativity.

We want to tell you that no great corporation, no great agency, no great business can flourish under a shadow of fear.

At some point in the life cycles of our agencies, we have all ruled by fear because we were fearful ourselves. It was so easy to settle into this constant state of worry. We wanted everything to go perfectly, and we panicked if it didn't. We also weren't great at hiding this anxiety and doubt from our teams. We barked orders and used "just because" as a reason to do certain activities.

As you might guess, not only were these micromanaging, fear-based management styles unappealing to our staff, but they also didn't exactly lead to accelerated growth.

It was a tough lesson, but at some point, we finally learned this fundamental truth:

It's when you let go that you begin to grow.

Dictator bosses get things done… for a while. But in the end, they find themselves constantly refilling a dwindling roster of average players, wondering why no one seems to be able to "get the job done."

Great environments are not fear-based. Rather, they are built upon trust, respect, and positive encouragement.

THE POINTLESS PURSUIT OF PERFECTION

You can have the sharpest, most talented employees in the world, but when you boil it down, the only person who can ultimately determine the environment is you, the agency owner.

We've found that to be both a good thing and a challenge.

It's a good thing because it gives you the power to change your environment for the better—but it also means that if you are prone to being a control freak or if you insist on having everything done a certain way, you could come across as a dictator, not a leader.

Jumping onto every mistake will quickly wear your team down. It will make them fearful of making errors of any kind. They won't be empowered to take a chance or go out on a limb for a client because they'll be worried about getting in trouble.

They definitely won't go the extra mile for clients—that would require them to think outside the box, a practice that is forbidden in a dictatorship.

It seems that our society as a whole is so focused on pointing out mistakes that our creativity is becoming collectively suppressed. The smallest mistakes made by business leaders, politicians, religious leaders, and celebrities are instantly on display for the world to see, sending the message that mistakes will not be tolerated.

Only ridiculed and punished.

Nothing could be more counterproductive. When an employee who is genuinely trying makes a mistake, the worst thing you can do is come down hard, use the person as an example of what not to do, or constantly remind this agent of his error.

If you think you are helping someone by pointing out his or her failings in front of the rest of the team, you are mistaken. Doing so will only lead that team member to feel isolated and distrustful.

Mistakes are not something to be ashamed of, nor should they ever be instruments of manipulation used to scare people into better performance.

Zappos CEO Tony Hsieh once tweeted about a $1.6 million mistake that an employee had made while updating prices on their website. Because of the glitch, for an entire day, no item for sale on Zappos.com cost more than $49.95. Since they have many products with price tags in the hundreds and even thousands of dollars, this was a pretty painful mistake.

When asked about whether he immediately fired the person for making such a grievous error, here was Hsieh's response:

"To those of you asking if anybody was fired, the answer is no, nobody was fired—this was a learning experience for all of us. Even though our terms and conditions state that we do not need to fulfill orders that are placed due to pricing mistakes, and even though this mistake cost us over $1.6 million, we felt that the right thing to do for our customers was to eat the loss and fulfill all the orders that had been placed before we discovered the problem."

What a great way to handle mistakes in business! Instead of calling out the guilty party, you can take the opportunity to show the true colors of your environment.

By doing this you can effectively create a paradigm shift in the way you and your employees view mistakes! In fact, rather than stigmatizing failure, you can actually use failures to make your agency even better by displaying integrity, understanding, and a humble attitude.

After all, mistakes are simply proof that you're trying.

In the absence of criticism and micromanagement in our agencies, you will now find agents who have the authority to override certain procedures or rules in order to do what is best for the client.

Will they make a few mistakes? Sure. But since that is unavoidable, and you can't work alone and achieve top agency status, why fight it?

An empowered employee is the kind of person you want representing your agency, not a fearful order taker who anxiously awaits the next "motivational" speech about how one more mistake will be the end of the line.

The bonus to approaching mistakes in a positive light is that when you take the time to help them, coach them, and retrain them—rather than just calling out the mistake and moving on—you send the message that you have their back no matter what.

CELEBRATION VERSUS CONDEMNATION

When we started treating mistakes in a more enlightened manner, we all noticed massive shifts in positivity, work ethic, and results. Those kinds of results prompted us to establish a new philosophy in our agencies:

"Catch someone doing something right."

Since mistakes are inevitable, we have found that the best course of action is to instead point out the positive. In our agencies, emails go out at the end of the day with subject lines such as "Congratulations to Jill" rather than "Still Behind on Monthly Quota."

Celebrate victories daily—not monthly, or even weekly. You have to celebrate your staff far more than you criticize them. Celebrating positives will always lead to more positives.

The insurance industry has a steep and intimidating learning curve that can become too much for many new recruits to overcome. Celebrating baby steps on the way up that curve is often the only way to keep them inching forward.

When (not if) someone makes a mistake, it's not only okay, but it's also an excellent learning opportunity. As salespeople, we know that an objection is a prospect's way of saying, "I'm still not sure about this." In the same way, a mistake made by an employee who is genuinely trying really means, "I need more training in this area" or "Refresh me on the procedures for this."

That is a key teaching moment—and in many cases, it's a teaching moment for you, too. It shows you where your training and onboarding process might need some work.

As a general rule, we try to point out a minimum of six positive things for every corrective comment. We also let our teams know that making course corrections will have exponential results on their bottom line, and then we *show* them how to do it better the next time.

Confusion and frustration do not lead to good outcomes. They can also breed a lack of confidence in your leadership. Make sure you are focused on creating a positive training environment that allows your staff to thrive.

We all make mistakes and will continue to make them. Don't focus on those. Instead, keep an eye out for the exceptional. Watch out for the extra-mile activities and celebrate them. Throw a party. Make a big deal.

When the mistakes happen, teach from them, learn from them, and move on to the next win.

Nobody is perfect, and if you expect anyone to be flawless, you will be sorely disappointed. Salvador Dali once said, "Have no fear of perfection. You'll never reach it."

Rechannel
Your Energy

We are on a mission to change how our customers view insurance and to give people a "total client experience," not just so-so customer service.

Whether we realized it or not, this mission has always driven us. However, during the first few years of our agencies, there was one thing that was secretly sabotaging us that almost derailed the entire train.

Let's go back to the beginning. Do you remember the moment you decided to start your own agency?

If you're like we were, you were filled with anticipation, doubt, excitement, and a thousand other feelings all at once.

Not everyone is cut out to run his or her own business. Being a successful entrepreneur takes a special breed. One thing we've noticed is that most new agency owners are absolutely *full* of energy and drive.

Unfortunately, energy doesn't always translate into results. You can work 18 hours a day but still not succeed if you don't know how to go about getting the results you want.

In fact, that misplaced energy can actually cause problems.

We get it—you're naturally excited and nervous. You're running your own business! It's up to you to succeed or fail. That kind of pressure is enough to cause you to lose sight of some fundamentals.

For example, none of us has ever enjoyed being ruled by an iron fist, and yet, at some point in all of our careers, we've all led with attitudes that sound like, "I sign the checks around here, so if you don't do what I say, you're fired."

Do you know what that type of attitude does for an office?

Just enough.

You may be able to make a *little* money, but you will also find yourself waking up five years from now wondering why you still have to work so hard finding new customers and why your attrition rates—for both clients and employees—are so high.

Maybe you'll blame the economy or do what we did, which was to sweep things under the rug with, "I guess this is just the nature of insurance sales." But the reality is, when you lead with misplaced energy, you breed people who are afraid to go out on a limb for clients.

You foster people who never go that extra mile.

They often won't even go that extra step.

What you end up with is an office full of people who are so worried about making a mistake that they miss the big picture. They put policies and procedures above clients, and that is a foundation for failure.

There is a fantastic book you should read—or read again: *How to Win Friends and Influence People* by Dale Carnegie. One of our favorite pieces of advice reads, "Criticism is futile because it puts a person on the defensive and usually makes them strive to justify themselves."

At this point in your career, you've probably already figured out that motivation works better than criticism. Unfortunately, rechanneling your energy so that it becomes constructive rather than destructive is often an "easier said than done" situation. That's because when it's *your* business and *your* money on the line, there is a secret saboteur waiting in the wings.

That silent destructive force is your emotions.

It's no easy task to run your own business, and if you are losing money, fear can manifest in a million detrimental ways. That is when you subconsciously begin to project your emotions onto others.

During the first few years in our businesses, we thought we actually *wanted* our employees to be fearful. We wanted them to be worried and feel that pressure, because that's how *we* felt.

Does that make much sense? Not really—but that is simply the power that our emotions have. They can cause us to lose sight of what we know is best.

Would you want to work in an environment where you are constantly reminded that your job is on the line, and one false move is "lights out" for your career? That is tantamount to working in a war zone, with snipers behind every bush, who are just waiting for you to make one false step or stick your neck out too far for a client.

After operating with a sense of fear for a while, we eventually woke up and realized why we kept bleeding employees and failing to hit targets.

How can you cultivate and sustain consistent business when you have installed a revolving door for employees? The answer is simple. You can't.

We know it can be tempting to call in the troops for a "Come to Jesus" meeting where you lay down the law, letting them know just how serious the situation is and informing them that you will be forced to start firing people if they don't start performing.

This comes from a good place—you are driven. You want to feel that win. You're afraid you won't. So your emotions start to do the talking for you.

This intrinsic drive in us doesn't have to manifest itself in a negative way. In fact, it can lead to great feats, but only when it is guided by a purpose bigger than our own gain.

Imagine you are sitting on your front porch watching your son play catch with a friend. One toss goes sideways, and your son takes off after the ball. You look to the right, and you see a truck flying down the street at 50 miles per hour. In an instant you jump over the porch, hit the ground running, and head full speed into the street with no thought for your own safety. You grab your son and dive into the air to reach the other side of the road, as you feel the wind of the passing truck on your cheek.

What could have stopped you from flying off of that porch?

Nothing! And why? Because you were purpose driven.

When you're driven by a bigger purpose, little things like fear, worry, and self-doubt can't stop you.

WORKING TOWARD A COMMON GOAL

We know you have a bold and inspiring vision inside you or you wouldn't be reading this book. One way to retrain your energy and effectively build a constructive environment is to involve your team in that vision.

Wait, other people want to be a part of something big and exciting?

Hard to believe, but true.

The first step in achieving this is simple: *communicate*. Make your vision a part of training, not just some obligatory words in a mission statement on the wall or on your website. Share your three, five, and even ten-year goals with your team, and ask them what their goals are as well. How do they align? Where do they conflict?

The people who work *with* you—not *for* you—should feel like they are a part of the future of the agency, not just a cog in the wheel of your master plan.

One of the absolute best ways to convey this is to trust your people and then let them *know* you trust them by empowering them to make some decisions.

It's your job to clearly establish the vision and then give your team some authority to do what they feel is best for the client in minor situations. This is the only way they will ever feel like they are a part of that vision.

If you're like us, you want to breed people who are on a mission. We are on a mission to change how people see insurance and to give people a "total client experience," not just so-so customer service.

Why is this so important?

Because people want to go on a mission with other people.

People want to do something exciting.

They don't just want to go work—they want to join a movement.

If you want inspired action, and if you want people to work harder and longer for you because *they* want to, you've got to create an environment that runs on motivation and is driven by a set of unified goals.

On a truly united team, there is no single MVP. *Everybody* is important. To us, our team members are like parts of the body. Is the heart or the brain more important? You need both of them to survive, just as you need the role of every team member to propel your agency to new heights.

The real reason this works so well is that unity increases morale… morale boosts work ethic… better work ethic means more and happier clients… and happier clients mean everything.

If you have a big enough purpose and let others be a part of it, big things can happen.

You can also use common goals in place of fear as a motivator. For example, we know everyone loves to leave early on Fridays, so we offer the incentive of getting to leave early on the last Friday of the month if they hit a certain number *as a team* to make up for being behind on monthly targets.

Do you think they try their hardest to make that happen?

They do, every time. Even better, they usually end up *destroying* the goal and going way beyond.

If you want to change the environment in your office, find something everyone can rally around, something everyone can get excited about, because a team that is united behind a common goal can move mountains.

You must begin to work on rechanneling your energy and your drive into creating a more productive environment where people don't just come to work, they *love* coming to work (and yes, it's possible!).

Lead by Example

"Leaders should be good role models."

We've all heard that before.

It may be common sense, but that doesn't mean it's common practice.

There is no shortage of shocking public exposures of the latest CEO or business leader who turned out to be corrupt—Jamie Dimon of JP Morgan, Henry Paulson of Goldman Sachs, Kenneth Lay of Enron, and of course, Bernie Madoff, just to name a few.

Why should leaders be outstanding role models who lead by example? Beyond the ethical considerations, there's an exceedingly practical one:

It's effective.

If you're going to tell people to do certain things in certain ways, you need to be a living, breathing illustration of exactly the kind of agent you want *them* to be.

For example, if you are looking to create a positive sales and service environment, then make sure you are the first person to interact with clients when they walk through the door in order to show your staff what you expect of them.

Your clients should sense that this is an office where employees are happy—and that originates with you. It's also your job to make sure employees understand *why* you want to create that atmosphere for clients and for each other.

Your employees' actions directly affect your livelihood, but it's not just about the bottom line. Great coaches and teachers *care* about their players and their students, and one of absolute best ways to show your team that you care about them is to be amazing!

This doesn't have to be hard or complicated. Sometimes, what your team needs is for you to encourage them. This can be as simple as walking through your agency and personally thanking each team member for his or her unique contributions.

Don't send a thank you email; say it in person!

Looking someone directly in the eyes and saying, "I'm glad you're a part of our team. Thank you for what you do," can have a huge impact on a staff member's outlook regarding your agency and your leadership.

YOUR FIRST JOB IN THE MORNING

One of the biggest issues we noticed at the helm of our businesses was that the lowest points of our agencies—the times of underperformance and steep agent and client attrition—came after our teams lost their motivation and excitement.

What happened during those times? They lost their excitement because we had lost ours!

These were times when we would dump our business woes onto the shoulders of those around us, and they hated it. And they *performed* like they hated it. We had to make a conscious decision to change this "attitude dump." That is when we finally woke up and realized:

If I want to change my business, I have to change myself.

The great Zig Ziglar said it this way, "If you want to change the output, you have to change the input." At some point in our careers, we consciously chose to shut down the negativity in our minds. One of the best ways to accomplish this is by listening to or reading something uplifting in the morning. It's also ideal to do this at bedtime.

When you consistently put positive messages in, that's exactly what comes out.

Your agency employees will only be as excited and motivated as you are. Positive feelings, motivation, and excitement always flow from the top down. The next time you walk into the office, are you going to set a positive tone or a negative one?

Over the years, and especially after one of our motivational keynote talks, we've heard people say things like, "I'm all for motivation, but it just doesn't last."

Imagine their surprise when we tell them, "We agree!"

Motivation doesn't last forever. As Zig Ziglar said, "Motivation is like bathing. That's why we recommend it daily."

Inspiration isn't something you can tap into once and get your fill for life. You've got to work on it every single day.

Keep that in mind the next time you see a member of your staff struggling with negativity. Without a daily—and in some cases, hourly—dose of inspiration, negativity is actually the normal state of being for most people.

That is why you've got to be their inspiration!

Imagine an old friend gives you a call one morning. You exchange greetings and then he says, "I just wanted to tell you a few things. First of all, you mean so much to me. You've been such a positive influence in my life. I wish I had more friends like you, because most people I know are negative. But whenever I talk to you, I feel encouraged. I feel like I can do anything because of you. I thank God every day for putting you in my life. Look, I know you're busy; I just wanted to call and tell you that. Have a good day."

Then he hangs up without even giving you a chance to respond.

Is it possible that the rest of your day might be a little better? Do you think you might be able to walk into your office with your head held high and a skip in your step? There is no doubt you'll have a smile on your face, and chances are good you'll feel particularly inspired to do exceptional work that day.

The funny thing is, your friend didn't teach you how to be a better salesperson or leader, did he? He certainly didn't teach you anything about insurance.

Your friend didn't increase your ability one bit. All your friend did was to tell you how great he thought you were. He handed you the gift of motivation and helped you believe in yourself.

How powerful is that message? We don't get that enough from the people around us. It is the exact same thing for your employees, prospects, and customers.

As a whole, people are more negative than they are positive. Unfortunately, that means the majority of the messages your employees receive every day from the world, from their friends, and even from their families are negative.

You can help change that. You can make it your personal mission to be the positive voice in your employees' ears. You can be someone they believe in and who they know believes in them.

You can make it your first duty each and every day to inspire the people in your life.

You can be that friend who tells them they have greatness inside of them. You can be that friend who tells them they can do anything, who reminds them that anything is possible.

Try waking up 30 minutes earlier in the morning to read something positive, and then share the most important points about what you read in a group email to your team. When your employees get to work, they will know that the first thing they'll see in their inbox are words of inspiration and encouragement from their leader.

If you think your employees won't read it or such a task isn't worth your time, then maybe you are right. People often rise to meet our exact expectations; so expect them not to care and they probably won't.

But believe amazing things can happen by daily inspiring your team, and maybe, just maybe, they will.

Treat your employees as more than just a human resource. Don't make working late on a regular basis an expectation. Don't ask them to come in on Saturdays unless *they* want to. Treat them right and build them up through your words and actions, and you'll see inspired work and explosive growth.

FOSTER ACCOUNTABILITY

The best agency environments are highly conducive to accountability—and this accountability starts at the top. If you tell your staff you will do something or help them with something, you *must* follow through on that promise.

This is the only way you can gain the credibility you need to *inspect what you expect* within your agency.

When it comes to following up on assignments, don't ask a question like, "How did it go today?" Instead, make it specific, such as, "What happened with the Jones deal?"

Being specific lets them know that when they commit to something, not completing it is *not* an option. By doing this, you're setting a tone and fostering an environment that values follow-through.

Following up isn't only about expectation; it's also a chance to assist the staff. In our agencies, we don't make following through a one-man or one-woman show. We may have three to four brief meetings a week with certain agents dedicated to following up with prospects who have expressed interest but have not yet purchased a policy.

> ## ASA TIP
>
> If you say you are going to do something, you better move heaven and earth to get it done. If you don't follow through, neither will your staff.

The main purpose of those meetings is to assist; it's all about how we can help our agents.

When employees become a part of your team, they are looking to *you* for training and mentoring. That is why you shouldn't consider this kind of follow-up to be micromanagement. Rather, you can choose to see it as your responsibility to your team to help them achieve their goals.

Ultimately you want to create an expectation in employees that you, their leader, are willing to help them succeed in any way you can.

If you have children or even nieces or nephews, you obviously want them to succeed. You want them to get good grades in school and obey their teacher. It would be irresponsible not to set standards and expectations, then hold those children accountable to them.

When you have to discipline them for doing wrong, that doesn't mean you don't care about them. As a matter of fact, you must discipline and correct to show that you *do* care about them.

Similarly, if you truly care about someone's professional well-being, you will do everything you can to help develop them, including setting expectations, defining standards, and holding them accountable for living up to them.

Sometimes you're going to have tough conversations. But you can do it in a way that lets them know how much you care. Turn the moment into a teaching opportunity and avoid being critical.

RESPECT AND BE RESPECTED

Do you know the best ways to earn the respect of your employees? Is it hands-on training? Maybe it's more incentive programs? Actually, earning their respect has nothing to do with gimmicks, rewards, or games. Rather, it is based on being the kind of leader you'd want leading you.

If you want respect, first and foremost you have to give it with no expectations or qualifications. You can also show your team you respect them by:

- Exhibiting sincere gratitude for their hard work, their resilience after rejection, and their ability to learn from mistakes.
- Doing what you say you are going to do. If you commit to something, come through on your end of the deal.
- Offering your assistance. Go out of your way to help people when it seems like they need it, especially if it isn't required of you.

- Being a good listener and respecting the opinion of others, even if you don't agree.
- Getting to know your employees on a personal level and never judging a book by its cover.
- Never engaging in derogatory talk about others in the office. Even if you and a team member seem like you are bonding over discussing another employee, you will lose all credibility as a trustworthy person in that team member's mind.

When you engage in respectful treatment of your employees, they will work harder for you. They will also pay it forward to customers. By performing the same actions you want to see in them, they will learn from you and mirror those actions almost instinctively.

Employees don't care how much you know *until they know how much you care*. That doesn't mean you have to get extremely personal with them; only that you should display a genuine concern about what's going on in their lives. People who see and feel that you care will respect you and work harder.

A big part of fostering an environment of mutual respect is keeping open lines of communication. Employees have to know they can come talk to you about issues or concerns, and you must be able to talk to them as well.

Sweeping things under the rug is simply not an option.

Address things immediately; your swift action will subconsciously convey respect and keep bad attitudes from festering and damaging your agency environment.

Open lines of communication also mean you remain open to discussing new ideas. Do you think you're the only one with ideas for growing your agency? No way. Some of the best ideas can come from unlikely sources.

The Wright brothers weren't engineers; they were bicycle shop owners. Masking tape was invented by a guy who worked for an auto body paint shop.

Some of the best ideas aren't totally out-of-the box or brand-new thoughts, but a combination of two or more established ideas. It's not always a brand-new idea or product that revolutionizes life, but the mixing of ideas to create a semi-new category of something amazing.

If you implement even one part of an employee's idea, that team member will be a million times more likely to apply it. So, embrace new ideas and encourage them.

Support Your
Second Family

T he alarm goes off at 5:30 A.M. and you are up for a quick run. After you shower, dress for success, and groom, you go downstairs to see your family and grab your morning coffee.

By 7:00 A.M., kisses and hugs have been exchanged, and you are out the door and on the way to your office. The day goes by in its usual flurry of activity—helping people, interviewing, and prospecting. It's a great day.

You get home a little after 6:00 P.M. and sit down to dinner with your girlfriend/boyfriend or your spouse and children. If you have little ones, then after bath time, pajamas, and stories, it's off to bed for the kiddos.

By 8:30 P.M., you and your partner can sit back and talk and watch a few minutes of TV. And by 10:00 P.M. you doze off into dreamland, fueling up to do it all again tomorrow.

Let's do the math:

If you add up the actual amount of face time you have with your family each day, on a good day, it averages around *three hours of quality time*; that is, two hours with your kids and another hour with your spouse/partner.

On the other hand, you spend an average of *eight to ten hours a day at work.*

If work is where we spend the majority of our time, then we have to treat each other like family. Family doesn't mean we become best friends, but it does mean we come together and support each other in achieving our goals. Many successful sports teams consist of players who don't always love (or even like) all their teammates, but when they take the field, they become one unit.

They become a team, because the end goal is to win, and coming together is the only way to accomplish that.

One great way to strengthen camaraderie among employees is to reward the team as a unit. We like to pay bonuses to everyone on the team when the office collectively reaches an agency-wide goal. This creates a competitive, yet supportive environment; if someone is not stepping up, others will try to lift that team member up.

It's easy to overlook one or two of your players in the pursuit of growing your business. If you have an unproductive employee, try connecting with that person on a personal level. Get to know him or her, and you may discover that the root of the problem has nothing to do with skill level.

If you want to create an all-star environment that motivates people to go above and beyond, do their best, and support one another, you must remember this:

Just as our clients are more than sales, our employees are more than their numbers.

Get to know every employee on a personal level. Always have an open door. They should know they can come talk to you about a personal matter affecting their performance—without being judged or made to feel like their job is on the line.

The only caveat to this rule is to be diligent in making sure lines never get crossed. There is a limit to how much personal information should be shared at the office. Crossing that line will break down your agency's perceived level of professionalism, both with clients and within the community.

Leaving the complications of business relationships aside, the bottom line is this: Respect people, learn what they need, and provide it as best you can—this will lead them to work harder, because people know how rare it is to find leaders who care enough to allow them to do what they need to do.

Care about your people and see what happens.

If it helps, picture your employees wearing a big button that says, "I am important. Ask me about my day." This mindset accomplishes several things:

1. It enables you to see your team members as human beings, not worker bees.
2. It reminds you to tell individuals that you appreciate them on a regular basis and to find out if there's anything you can do for them.
3. It allows you to stop and listen for teachable moments within the environment. These moments can come from both positive and negative activity, but each is very important, as is the way you handle them.

It's incredibly easy to find staff members doing something wrong, but *it's your job to find them doing something right.* So, reach out. Make them feel like the family member they are.

Hold a monthly lunch (your treat), shut the office down for an hour, and enjoy fellowship with each other. Invite staff members to bring a special dessert to share with the team. Host a Thanksgiving dinner where everyone brings in a dish to celebrate the Wednesday before the holiday together.

This is your extended family, so treat them as such! If they feel like family, then they'll act like family, which means they won't always be perfect. But they will be loyal—and that's a priceless and rare gift.

VOLUNTEERING AS A TEAM

Few things bond people together like volunteer work. If you've ever volunteered to help build a home, serve up lunch in a soup kitchen, or collect clothes or toys for kids, you know little else can make you feel so warm inside.

Now imagine doing those things with your colleagues.

Every month, we close our offices for two to three hours to go out and volunteer as a unit. Even better, we invite customers to come with us. This accomplishes three things:

- First, it has made our staff look at us in a completely different light. All too often, sales leaders are seen as one-track-minded businesspeople who live to drive results. Why not show your human side and allow your team to see that you care about more than just financial performance?
- Second, it has increased their level of respect for the leadership team. They appreciate being given a regular opportunity to do

something for people in the community. This also helps give them a break from the grind of a fast-paced career in insurance.

- Third, it has changed the way clients view our agencies. We become more than "insurance agents." This encourages feelings of loyalty and gratitude, and it helps us stand out from the crowd.

After one of our volunteer events, you can actually *feel* the change in the office environment. The energy that comes from helping others is unmatched in its ability to inspire and motivate.

Another great way to band together using charity work is to start a donation program. You can combine charitable work with good business practices by creating a referral program that supports your clients' favorite cause. If a client provides you with a referral, you can donate $10 or another amount to a charity in that client's name.

The result is a triple-win—the client receives recognition for helping your agency support a good cause, the cause benefits from the donation, and your agency has just gained a qualified lead.

THEIR 'OTHER' FAMILIES

Although we may spend more actual time at work, most people say their family is their top priority. In fact, if we had our way, we'd spend a whole lot more time with our loved ones than the modern, breakneck work pace allows.

In this country, we send our kids off to daycare or school and spend a few quality minutes with our family each day. Weekends fly by in a blur, so much so that we feel like we blink and it's back to work again on Monday.

Now imagine you told your employees that they are free to attend their kids' activities, games, or performances without ever having to ask permission. They just need to tell you what days they'll be gone and when or how they'll make up the time.

How do you think that would make them feel?

In a word—thankful. So many workplaces require people to use vacation and sick days just to see their kids' events and programs.

If you want to promote a family-like environment, you've got to value people's commitment to their families.

Christmas parties are another great opportunity to involve families and spouses. In fact, we like to recognize the staff's significant others formally at holiday functions. It's important to make sure family members feel that you value and appreciate how hard their loved one is working for your agency.

Never underestimate the power of ingratiating yourself to your employees' spouses. Gaining their support is of the utmost importance, because there are going to be times when staff members will need to work late, and spouses often have a hard time with that.

They need to understand this business. They need to understand that you appreciate their spouse, and them, as well!

Holiday parties are a great time to tell employee family members how important they are to the success of the agency. Invite family to functions beyond the Christmas party, such as the volunteer projects.

Paint a vision for them of where the agency is going, how they are going to be a part of it, and how you cannot grow without them. If you plan to expand, make them a part of it. Give them a piece of the pie.

Your work family matters—they are the people with whom you spend more time than anyone else, so why not make them feel as special as they are?

||||||

Each and every waking moment, you have the opportunity to shape and mold your agency's environment to your desired specifications. If you want people to *love* doing business with you, and if you want a team of superstars who *love* coming to work, then you should:

1. Let go of the endless pursuit of perfection. Catch employees doing something right and celebrate achievements rather than criticize mistakes.
2. Rechannel your energy and emotions into working toward a common goal and promoting team unity.
3. Choose your agency's attitude by promoting positive talk, rewarding results, encouraging healthy competition, dressing for success, shutting down negativity, and fostering a fun environment.
4. Create a relationship-driven agency by viewing customers as people rather than transactions. Encourage the use of networking and lead with the "why" in training by explaining the client-focused purpose of what you are teaching them.
5. Lead by example by living what you talk, motivating through action rather than words or discipline, holding yourself and others accountable, and giving respect.
6. Treat employees like family. Take the time to get to know what is most important to them, care for their families, and volunteer together as a team.

Do all this, and you'll create an environment that attracts top talent and loyal customers. Dictatorships don't work. When you signed up for business ownership, it didn't give you a license to rule over others.

You are now, more than anything, a mentor and a motivator—and to be a great motivator, you must first motivate yourself. It is only when you successfully motivate yourself that you are able to motivate others.

So, go out there, seek daily inspiration, pass the inspiration along to your team, and watch your environment transform into a wealth of positivity and encouragement.

R

REVENUE

Distinguish Frantic Activity from Action

"If you build it, he will come."

Y ou may recognize this quote from the iconic 1989 film *Field of Dreams,* starring Kevin Costner.

If you haven't seen the film, or to refresh your memory if it's been a while, Costner's character, Ray Kinsella, is a struggling Iowa farmer who seeks peace regarding his troubled relationship with his deceased father, John, who had been a devoted baseball fan.

While walking in his cornfield one evening, Ray hears a voice telling him to "build it" and "he" would come. Not even knowing who "he" was, Kinsella builds a baseball field where his corn once was, much to the scorn of skeptics and naysayers.

And yet, by the end of the film, we are watching a literal fantasy game where long-since-passed baseball players such as Shoeless Joe Jackson play on this "Field of Dreams."

In the final scene, a younger version of Ray's father appears on the field, and Ray finally knows *that* is why he was supposed to build the field. He and his ghost dad play a game of catch while Ray's daughter watches, and the audience gets a warm, fuzzy feeling of closure.

The scene fades as we see hundreds of cars coming up the long drive, all of which we can assume are filled with people who are going to pay big money to watch some dead guys play baseball.

Now, you may be asking yourself, what does this have to do with growing your revenue?

In our experience, making a plan to "build revenue" doesn't work that well. Yes, that's the end goal—but it doesn't tell you how to get there. Focusing only on your bottom line will lead to *frantic activity*, stress, and frustration.

However, when you build your business around *focused action*, the revenue naturally follows. In other words:

If you build it (the right way), the revenue will come.

What are these actions that naturally generate the "revenue of your dreams?"

In this section, we will highlight the right activities that lead to accelerated growth and the revenue you want and deserve.

MAKING GOOD CHOICES EVERY SINGLE DAY

Is your revenue increasing every year?

If not, you should be asking why.

How often do you take a hard look at the amount of money you're netting every month?

You must answer these questions, and you must have a solid grasp on your financial situation to create the resources required to accomplish the most important things in your business; whether it's investing, hiring, purchasing technology, marketing, or simply having enough money to retire one day.

Revenue is critical to any business for obvious reasons, but what seems less obvious is figuring out how to maximize it. That part takes tremendous consideration and a well-planned strategy—both about how you best *utilize* the resources already available to you, and how you grow and *maximize* those resources.

Before we get into specific actions we implemented in our agencies that have significantly boosted revenue, let's talk about the one simple, overarching principle that encompasses every action you take:

Make good decisions.

> ## ASA TIP
>
> Focusing on the bottom line is ineffective because it doesn't relate to your why. Remember, money is just the means to achieve your *real* goals.

It seems simple. And yet it's so hard.

Making good decisions doesn't mean you avoid risk; avoiding risk in business is impossible. It simply means that whether you're hiring another person, investing in marketing or technology, calling on new prospects, following up with existing ones, or servicing a claim, you must approach every step with careful consideration and treat every single dollar like it's *the* most important object on the planet.

If there is something you don't absolutely need, and your agency doesn't have a lot of excess capital, then don't buy it. No further discussion needed.

Question every purchase and every financial decision made in your agency and be sure it's the right one. At the same time, never be afraid to invest in your agency, particularly when it comes to people. Seek out wise investments instead of using a dollar-amount-only litmus test for spending.

Many agency owners view "investing" as "spending." Avoid this mindset at all costs. Instead view expenditures on behalf of your business as investments, particularly when it comes to your staff. You want to make good decisions, but you also want to make the *right investments*, instead of operating just to avoid risk.

Over the next few chapters, we are going to uncover the actions that you can take to explode your revenue. First, we'll talk about your budget and other key ways to maximize revenue.

We'll then reveal *the one thing that is more important to your revenue than anything else*. It's something you can influence today, right now, no matter where you are in the life cycle of your agency.

If you build your business through the right actions, the revenue *will* come. It's one thing to talk about "making more money." It's another to take the steps necessary to ensure that you build your agency upon a foundation that encourages growth and lasting success.

Imagine how incredible it would feel to look at your net revenue at the end of the year and get excited.

Imagine knowing exactly how many dollars you'll get back for every dollar you spend.

You *can* and *will* experience those feelings by taking the steps provided in the pages that follow.

Budget and
Build Wisely

W hen you hear the words "tight budget," what comes to mind? Watching every penny, operating with a skeleton crew, and making calls in the dark? Or maybe you envision something not quite so extreme.

In our experience, we've found a tight budget is less about being a penny pincher and more about developing a *deep awareness* of your spending.

In this chapter, we will uncover those things that every agency owner must acknowledge, measure, and manage when it comes to your most liquid yet essential commodity.

You are probably familiar with the term "return on investment" or ROI. It is the most common profitability ratio used in business. There are several ways to determine ROI, but the most frequently used method is to divide net profit by total assets.

Return on investment isn't the same as profit. ROI deals with the money you invest in the company and the return you realize on that money based on the net profit of the business.

Let's say you invest in some new technology that has a high price tag, and that technology causes your revenue to grow exponentially. It'd be worth every penny, right?

That is why budgeting is less about "Spend fewer dollars!" and more about "What's the ROI on every dollar I'm spending?"

Rather than just look at a dollar amount, question everything—from your CRM software to every hire you make—and determine the ROI of each potential cash outflow.

Here is how that might work:

Let's say you are considering investing in a VoIP (Voice over Internet Protocol) system. You've talked to other agency owners who are using one, and you think it might be worth the investment.

If you want to grow your revenue, it's not just about bringing in new revenue; it's about keeping the money you've already made! So, when it comes figuring out whether or not this technology is a smart investment, ask yourself questions such as:

- Will I be able to fully utilize this technology?
- What is it about our current system that necessitates this new purchase?
- Are its extra features worth the difference in price tag compared to a traditional phone system?
- What will the new system provide that will make it worth the extra monthly expenditure?
- How will I train my people to use this system?
- Does my team want to learn a new system?

- How much time will it take to learn this new system?
- Do I have the time and resources to train them properly?

Don't even think about spending a dime on new technology or a new hire until you put pen to paper and work out the numbers. Then, after the new purchase is in place, work the numbers again to ensure you made the right decision.

Some expensive investments are worth it. Just be careful about making high-dollar purchase after purchase, especially when capital is low. You'll end up with too little profit and eventually, spiraling debt.

For the most part—and particularly in the early stages of your agency—focus on new business opportunities that don't cost a lot of upfront money. Examples include regularly asking for referrals and actively building centers of influence.

You may have heard the phrase, "You have to spend money to make money," and that's true, to a point. But don't use that as an excuse to buy brand new laptops and designer office furniture for every workspace.

Work the numbers, spend wisely, and find ways to get the most out of your business that won't break the bank.

HIRE ANOTHER SET OF EYES

Do you use a bookkeeper or a tax advisor to examine your expenses on a regular basis?

The vast amount of expenditures running through your agency makes it important to have another set of eyes on your expenses. A paid professional with no direct ties to your agency can help by objectively questioning why you bought something, or why you paid what you did for a service.

The right bookkeepers are trained to find the holes in a business where money is leaking out. There are many times when our book-keepers have informed us of such holes. Maybe it was a forgotten subscription that needed to be cancelled, office supplies that were unnecessary, or unqualified leads that warranted refunds.

That's correct—there are some lead-provider services that will reimburse you for dead-end leads. Do you have a foolproof process to ensure that you get credit for every lead that is not a valid contact?

If not, you should. This alone could add a few hundred dollars to your bottom line every month. You may be leaving money on the table due to a process that needs to be refined.

We meet with our bookkeepers regularly. They question everything, poking and prodding to make sure we are making the right investment decisions for our businesses. They compare the prior month to the current month, as well as year-to-date versus the previous year-to-date.

At fiscal year-end, we meet with our bookkeepers and accountants to make sure expenses are still in line. Then we set budget goals for the upcoming year.

All the wise spending and tracking in the world won't accelerate your growth if you are being bled dry by employees who are costing more money than they are generating. So, let's return again to a brief discussion of the cost of making a wrong hire.

MONEY-MAKERS VS. MONEY-TAKERS

A wrong hire can become one of the biggest revenue-draining entities in your business. We call the wrong hire a *money-taker*. Your goal is to steer clear of them and instead hire *money-makers*. No matter who you hire, the costs of hiring are great. Here are some of the most obvious costs associated with the hiring process:

1. **Advertising.** There are ongoing advertising costs associated with attracting new candidates.

2. **Your Time.** You spend time conducting interviews, not to mention the time it takes to evaluate candidates and their personality profiles. What is your time worth to the agency?

3. **Other Employees' Time.** You have to pull managers or other trusted employees away from their work to help with staff interviews. Others help during training and onboarding. What is their time worth?

4. **Training and Onboarding Time.** The initial training period lasts up to 90 days, a period during which a new employee typically makes limited contributions to your bottom line. There's also ongoing development after the training period ends.

5. **Loss of Sales During Training.** While someone is training, he or she is not selling. When you or a sales manager take three to four hours out of your day to train a new hire, your sales are going to take a hit as well. What do you think that does to your revenue?

6. **New Hires Burning Through Leads.** During training, you put an unqualified person into the field to start prospecting and selling to qualified prospects. The new hire will naturally miss opportunities that a more seasoned agent would not. Now you have lost opportunity cost. Multiply that by 90 days and come up with an uncomfortably large number.

7. **Salary/Draw During Training.** Don't forget to add any salary or draw you paid new people over the first 90 to 180 days.

8. **Influence on Others.** If you make the wrong hire, a money-taker may potentially be a negative influence in your agency, which could cause productivity issues with other team mem-

bers. Be protective of your people and protect their attitudes by not bringing in new employees who are negative, lazy, or inept.

How can you avoid hiring a money-taker? It's not always possible; some do slip through the cracks and land in our agencies. However, we have drastically reduced the number of bad hires in our agencies by following the ten-step hiring process presented in Part I.

When the occasional money-taker does surface on our teams, we are always quick and decisive in handling them. They don't stick around long.

If you can eliminate those candidates during the interview process who would eventually drain your revenue, you will save yourself valuable time that can be spent creating revenue-generating opportunities you would have missed had you made the wrong hire.

> ### ASA TIP
>
> |||||||||||||||||||||||||||||||||||||||||||||||
>
> We will not hesitate to let a money-taker go. We're not running charities. We are in business to make money. Stand up for your agency and cut the money-takers loose.

The difference between a money-maker and a money-taker is enormous for your agency and its bottom line. Spend a few dollars on a personality profile such as Ideal Traits and get to know your new hires; the cost of testing is more than worth it.

Your business will thrive on money-makers. So, pay attention to payroll and see if you're getting a solid ROI from each individual. If your return on investment is meager, you need to make some different decisions.

DUPLICATE YOURSELF

Even if you are careful and take your time in the hiring process, your new hires will only be as good as their training allows. What is one way to ensure you are getting the best ROI when it comes to your employees?

The answer is to duplicate yourself.

Gary Keller, founder of the real estate company Keller Williams, wrote in his book *Shift* that he is proud of the fact that they only hired a handful of people when he started his now multi-billion-dollar business. He didn't put the cart before the horse. He didn't hire as many bodies as he could. Instead, he carefully hired the right people, who then hired the right people, who then hired the right people, and so on.

You cannot expect to run a well-organized, high-revenue organization without a commitment to having upbeat, positive, motivated individuals working together toward a common goal. And the best way to build a winning a team of like-minded individuals is to teach them exactly how you want things done.

Don't leave it up to chance or assume they'll magically know how you want them to talk to customers, prospect, and represent your agency and your brand.

Create a legion of duplicates—agents who know exactly what to do because you *showed* them exactly what to do.

At one of our live events, an agency owner told us, "I'll always be the top writer in my agency and the one bringing in the most revenue. I'm not leaving my fate up to someone else."

We've felt this way before, too. We told him what we all had to admit at some point in our agencies, and that is:

"This line of thinking will stunt the growth of your agency and stifle the activity required to create a revenue generating machine."

Although it sounds like a good idea to always be the point-person for your clients, you simply cannot handle all your customers' needs if you want to experience accelerated growth.

We learned that duplicating ourselves increases our agencies' potential by putting the right people in place with the right skills. We can accomplish service goals by taking care of customers in a timely fashion, and at the same time, we can take big leaps toward the goal of growing our businesses.

||||||

The most lucrative agencies run lean in both good times and bad. Running lean is not just about watching your pennies; it's not just about keeping the perfect number of agents aboard at all times.

It's about making sure you're paying people the right amount of money for the value they bring to your agency.

It's also about setting up a system of checks and balances to help you understand how each dollar is performing, and duplicating yourself so that your agency runs efficiently, with or without you in the office.

Don't Bench
the Star Player

Would you like to make money while you're sleeping?

Unlike most other professions, you're in an industry where this is *actually* possible.

"The easiest money you'll ever make is the money you're already making." That's a quote from one of our mentors, and it changed the way we looked at not only our insurance businesses but also business in general.

The insurance profession is one of the greatest trades on the planet—and this is because of the residual revenue potential. We know so many business owners who only *wish* they had a business structure that enabled them to receive money continuously from the same clients, year after year.

"Residual revenue" sounds great, but if you aren't focused on the right numbers, you won't reap the benefits of this industry perk. In the next few chapters, you'll discover that most of the revenue-boosting activities we will discuss are focused on a much more helpful, over-arching goal:

Grow your retention rate.

Increasing your retention rate will lead to huge amounts of residual revenue. That is why we call the retention rate the "star player," because it has such a big impact on your success.

And yet, the retention rate is a number to which many agency owners don't give enough attention. Instead, they focus on sales because *sales* equal new business. *Sales* are what win you all the awards. *Sales* are exciting. *Sales* are sexy. However, your sales are not the biggest factor.

If you can figure out how to increase your *retention*, it will accelerate your growth virtually overnight.

Increasing your retention rate is something that requires consistent attention, particularly as your agency develops. Every month, we recommend that you examine your one- to five-year retention numbers to see if there are certain actions or course corrections needed to improve them.

If you are focused solely on writing new business and ignore retention, it's going to cost you. You will end up spending a lot of unnecessary time and money chasing new business rather than taking advantage of what is right in front of you.

When our agencies were shedding clients and losing premium, we determined that the first thing we needed to do was to focus on the most important number—the retention rate. We started asking questions that every agency owner should ask, such as:

- What can I do to keep customers with me?
- What can I do to improve the client experience in order to foster loyalty?

- How can I turn each casual interaction into a relationship where clients understand that we truly care about them, so much so that they genuinely want to stick around?

By asking these simple questions, we got down to the root of the retention issue. Today, our agencies operate with extremely high retention rates—and that's pretty rare in our industry. A solid retention rate is also the number one reason our revenues are consistently high and continue to grow every day.

What did we do to produce such great retention rates?

That is what the next few chapters are about.

Now, since *we* know why you're reading this book, and *you* know why you're reading this book, there is no reason to sugarcoat it: we're all in business for one reason, and that is to make money.

We're also in business to serve. But without money, there would not be an agency and therefore no one to serve.

If you are looking to increase your revenue, don't start by thinking of new, clever ways to prospect or buying a book with 127 gimmicky closes.

> ## ASA TIP
>
> If you are serious about boosting your revenue, it may be time to shift your focus. Instead of making every goal about new sales, let your agents know how important the retention rate is—and then reward them for improving it.

We are going to share with you five focused actions you can take to increase retention and, as a result, your revenue.

If you believe you are in the *relationship* business rather than the *insurance* business, you can feel confident about actively pursuing a better retention rate to grow your agency and authentically serve more customers.

Create
Specialist Roles

As the fearless leader of your agency, you've got a lot on your plate. We can relate. As a group of leaders who had a hard time delegating tasks in the beginning stages of our businesses, we can verify that sometimes there is too much on our plates and not enough *us* to go around.

After years of experiencing customer attrition rates that were damaging our revenues, we figured out a few things. One of the first things we discovered is that staying on top of retention is not a part-time job; it's not something you can do between calls; it's not just a lunchtime activity.

It's a full-time job—and that means there must be roles within your agency that are devoted to nothing else. In this chapter, we'll describe the three roles we have created in our agencies to support the task of increasing customer loyalty.

RETENTION SPECIALIST

The first and most important position is what we call a *retention specialist*. This person's primary purposes are to perform the activities that directly support retention and foster a sense of allegiance to your agency. Here are two things to look for in this hire:

- **Great personality profile.** This individual must be outgoing, friendly, positive, upbeat, and should love dealing with people.
- **Organized.** The best hires for this role are extremely organized and consistent in their work ethic and actions.

Assign one person to be your champion for retention, and let this team member know that he or she is there for one reason—to make sure your clients stay with you for as long as they need insurance.

The Power of Auto-Draft. A few years into running our agencies, we noticed that a fair percentage of customers were consistently late in paying their monthly premiums, which was causing us to spend time chasing money we had already earned.

Studies show that you can increase your overall retention rate by 2 percent just from having clients enroll in automatic account draft (or auto-draft).[4]

What? A 2 percent increase in retention just for setting customers up on automatic payments? That should be a no-brainer in your business.

One of your retention specialist's primary tasks should be to get as many clients as possible on auto-draft. Role-play with this person and help him or her become highly skilled at having the "auto-draft conversation."

[4] http://www.dbmarketing.com/articles/Art232.htm

You can even set up a bonus structure for your retention specialist. For example, for every customer who moves from direct bill (where customers physically send in a check) to automatic draft, the specialist receives a $10 bonus.

Your clients will appreciate it as well because it saves them a stamp, and they don't have to worry about their premiums getting paid on time. On top of that, some insurance companies offer customers a discount for setting up an automatic payment.

The Power of Renewals. The next task to assign your retention specialist is to spearhead what we call the 45-Day Renewal Process.

Imagine how you would feel if you got a letter in the mail saying, "Remember how your monthly payment used to be $100? Well, now it's $150. Have a great day!"

That doesn't sound like such a great day—and yet, this is how your customers find out about rising premiums all the time.

Catching someone by surprise with bad news doesn't exactly foster loyalty. After losing too many customers because of this, we decided to make a change. We implemented a simple procedure called the 45-Day Renewal Process. Here's how it works:

We review every policy 45 days before it renews to find out whether the payment is going up, going down, or staying the same. If the premium is about to increase, we make it a point to contact our clients *before* they get a letter saying their premium is increasing.

If you notice a customer's price is going to increase, you have time to figure out what you can do to diminish the increase. You may even be able to find a way to keep those payments the same with minor tweaks in coverage amounts or new discounts.

Can you imagine someone going to bat for you like that? Can you imagine someone actually caring about your money and desiring to help you keep more of it? People would stand in line to do business with such a professional.

In our agencies, our goal is to find a solution before customers realize there's a problem.

It may make you feel uncomfortable to imagine deliberately calling clients to tell them their rate is going to increase. You might be thinking, "Why would I want to open up that can of worms?" We used to feel the same way, and we avoided the uncomfortable feeling that results from telling clients we'd be taking more of their money in the future.

People do not like surprises, but they can appreciate an explanation. Explain *why* their rate is increasing, and they will be grateful to you for taking time to clarify it and offering some solutions.

It's no small task to review every policy 45 days before renewal, which is why you need a retention specialist, someone who is dedicated to doing nothing other than retention-related activities.

We also task our customer service teams to be involved with retention, and a portion of their pay is based on their overall retention numbers. It's constantly on their minds, just as much as new business is for the sales manager and agents.

When you prioritize retention as highly as we do in our agencies, your employees won't be able to mistake it for an optional part of their success.

CLAIMS SPECIALIST

The next position is a claims specialist. Claims are the reason our business exists—they are the things our clients hope they never have to make, but they are certainly glad they have the ability to do so.

When a client has an accident or experiences fire or water damage and there's some kind of claim as a result, *that* is our moment of truth. We finally get to prove our worth in the client's eyes.

After big, unexpected events, most people are scared, worried, and unsure about the process—and they come to their insurance agents for help. What do a lot of agencies do? They tell clients to call an 800 number.

"Just give them a ring, ma'am. They'll take care of you."

When customers hear that, they think, "Let me get this straight. You sold me on how much you care about me and my well-being, but when the stuff hits the fan, I have to call customer service in India?"

We have all passed the buck at some point and pushed off the "problem" to someone else. Because it's easier; because new sales beckon; because on the surface, the thought of servicing a claim sounds like a misuse of our valuable time.

We've all been guilty of doing and thinking that.

How wrong we were.

When you treat claimants this way, you are making it too easy for customers to leave. Treating them like a number and passing along the responsibility of caring for them to someone else means there's no relationship.

You haven't done anything for them. Why should they be loyal?

Imagine, instead, hearing from your agent, "Come in and we'll start the process together. We're here for you. Whatever you need, just call. Here is my direct number."

After such an experience, that person will be a loyal and grateful customer for life. This is why you need at least one claims expert in your office, someone who knows the process well enough to be able to:

1. Comfort customers and be sensitive to what they are experiencing after they file a claim, especially since claims often arise out of traumatic experiences.
2. Walk people through the claims process and explain everything to them, including what will happen next.
3. Make sure they know they are in good hands and can continue to call the agency directly.

ASA TIP

Once the claims process is in motion, check with the customer at least once a week to make sure everything is going smoothly. Be their ally; they'll never forget it.

During a stressful time in their lives, you can be a source of help and reassurance. What a difference it makes to have a person who is committed and who walks through the whole process with you. We have gotten letters from clients thanking our claims specialists for the above-and-beyond assistance.

If you want to increase your retention and by extension your revenue, assign one person to be your claims warrior to fight *for* and *alongside* your clients.

POLICY TERMINATION SPECIALIST

The next retention support position is a policy termination specialist.

That's right. Just one person. For *all* policy terminations.

In the first years of our agencies, we allowed anyone to terminate policies. If a customer called and wanted to cancel a policy, we did what they asked, no questions asked.

None of us thought about trying to save those customers from leaving. On the surface, when a client wants to cancel, it seems like a problem—and who wants to deal with a problem?

We soon changed that mindset. Once we realized this was the wrong attitude, we came up with a new rule to remedy needless attrition: Train one person in your office to be the termination specialist. Any time a customer calls to cancel, or you receive notification that their policy is being cancelled, all roads lead to this designated employee.

This individual will subtly search to find the real reason for the cancellation and do his or her best to convince the customer that the best possible solution is to stay put.

Do we save them all? No. We save about 20 percent. Maybe you're thinking, "One in five? That's it?" By not having this type of process in place, you save no one. When you look at it that way, 20 percent is really impressive!

Consider incentivizing the specialist by paying $50 for every client saved. That may seem like a lot of money, but in the long run, it's not. The cost to acquire a new client is so much higher.

We encourage you to allow only one person (it could even be you) to have the authority to terminate policies. When you do that, it narrows the escape hatch people can use to leave your agency.

There is only one way out—through the termination specialist.

Do everything in your power to ensure clients' policies stay on the books. Create these specialist roles and get ready to see what increased retention can do for your bottom line.

Harness the Power of Annual Reviews

When you write new business, what do you do at the end of the deal? Do you thank your new customer and move on, already dreaming about the next big customer?

If so, you are overlooking a critical step that will bring untold amounts of revenue into your agency. Here is the missing step:

Every time we write new business, we verbally *set up the expectation that we'll be meeting with our clients each year to perform an annual review* in order to reassess their unique situation. With annual reviews, everyone wins:

- Your agency fosters loyalty and retention and has the opportunity to cross sell and upsell.
- Your clients feel confident that they have the right amount of coverage, and they have the opportunity to save money on their policies by reviewing them each year.

For our agencies, the annual review process has helped as much as 70 percent of our clients save money each year—something we let our new customers know at the beginning of the relationship.

We call the yearly meetings *Client Protection Reviews* (CPRs) because that's exactly what you are doing for the client by conducting them. You are also looking out for their best interests and making sure they have the *protection* they need.

Your customers are relationships, not transactions. So, make sure they receive every possible discount and understand their coverage.

Just as important as performing annual reviews with all customers is how you perform them. The process is critical. Here are the seven steps we take to ensure a successful Client Protection Review process:

1. Set Expectations

When new customers agree to buy a policy, let them know what they can expect from your agency. In our agencies, this includes telling them about our rapid response time for customer issues, our hands-on approach to handling claims, and our concierge programs that are full of local businesses outside the realm of insurance that have agreed to give our clients discounts or exclusive services (more on our concierge programs in Chapter 27).

Establishing expectations in the beginning sets you up for long and fruitful relationships with your customers, and it sets the stage for a successful review process, which we explain and lay out for them right from the start.

As their insurance agent, you are the second most important professional in their life. That's not ego; that's just fact. We protect the assets they've worked hard to grow, and we also help them build assets so they can retire with enough money to enjoy the rest of their lives without worry.

It's important that clients understand this; it gives your words and advice more footing moving forward.

2. Keep Control in Your Corner

Invite clients in for their review at least one month prior to their policy renewal date. After some small talk, begin the process by saying:

> "I noticed there are going to be some changes to your policy premiums. I know your budget is important to you, and I want to make sure you not only have the correct protection but also that we protect your budget."

It's ideal to use some sort of review guide sheet for the meeting that lists the questions and topics to cover. This will help you stay on track and, more importantly, *in control* of the meeting at all times. Clients with Type A personalities may try to control the appointment, and that can hurt your ability to get the most out of the review.

This is your chance to make sure they understand you are their Trusted Advisor, and you are there to make sure they have the right amount of coverage and are paying the right price. Using a guide will help you keep that control and keep the conversation on the right path.

For a sample version of an annual review form you can use, please visit: agencysalesacademy.com/growth.

3. Review Policy Details

After expectations have been set, it's time to discuss their policies. Make sure everything is accurate. Are they receiving all of their discounts? Do they understand their policy limits and what they're paying for every month?

Walk through all their coverages and protections. If they want to make tweaks because an increase is too high, you can do that. What's most important about this part of the process is the personal contact. You could do all of this over the phone, but it wouldn't be as effective.

With an annual review process, you can successfully get in front of those phone calls from customers that start with, "Why is my rate going up?"

You've no doubt been on the receiving end of a call like that before. It's a tough call to field; it puts you on the defensive, scrambling for an answer that usually isn't fast enough or good enough.

That is why we encourage you to solve problems before they arise.

One of the biggest reasons customers switch insurance agencies is premium increases. It makes sense when you consider that for most people, their policies don't take up much room in their minds on a daily basis. In fact, the only time we think about insurance is when we need it—or when our premiums increase.

To customers, our products are just some static numbers in their monthly budget. But once that price goes up, they notice, and it compels them to wonder if they should shop elsewhere. Prevent that trigger and catch the issue before it becomes a problem.

4. Ask the Million-Dollar Question

After you review their policies, rate changes, and discounts, next comes the million-dollar question, which is:

"So, tell me more about what you do for a living."

After you ask, sit back and make it about the client. Human beings are inherently self-centered. That's not necessarily a bad thing, but it's important to understand. People love to talk about themselves. We don't always get the opportunity with our circle of friends or even family to brag a little.

You *want* customers to brag about what they do. This is an interesting part of the review because you can learn a lot about people, and you can also get a lot of information—and information is power.

Ask about whether they like their job, what kind of benefits they have through their employer, and how long they think they'll be working there. Take notes so you won't forget the important things that pertain to potential life changes.

The new information you discover will allow you to advise them more accurately, help them save the most money possible, and ensure they have the right amount of coverage.

Listen intently, ask questions, and discover things you have in common with clients. When they form a sincere connection with you, that personal relationship will keep them loyal to your agency. It can also lead to more referrals, and that's always a good thing!

Now that you have found common ground, the next question to ask is:

"Before we get started and go over your policies in detail, do you have any questions I can answer for you?"

This is a pivotal moment that uncovers their real reasons for agreeing to come in for the annual review.

Most agents automatically assume that a customer agrees to come in only because of a rate increase, but that may not be true. There could be changes in their life or work that have created new concerns or opportunities they want to talk about. Or there could be specific issues they have with their insurance cover or recent claims experience. This question helps the agent gain confidence and stop worrying about an increase that the client may not even see as an issue.

5. Uncover Opportunities

Letting clients talk about themselves encourages them to re-engage in the conversation at the most important part of the annual review, which is discussing other policies they may need.

Most significant among these is an *umbrella policy*—a type of insurance that provides liability coverage over and above an automobile or homeowners policy. It protects your clients' valuable assets from an unforeseen event, such as a tragic accident for which they are held responsible for damages or bodily injuries.

We believe every customer should have an umbrella policy. However, it's not always easy or simple to convince customers of this. That is one of the reasons annual reviews are so effective. Explaining their existing policies' strengths and limitations is a powerful way to illustrate the need and true value of an umbrella policy.

At this point in the review, you can also tell them about any other coverages or financial services your agency offers. For more on uncovering opportunities, cross selling, and upselling, see the next chapter on turning your agency into a one-stop shop for all things related to insurance and finance.

6. Ask the Two Million-Dollar Question

As the annual review draws to a close, there is one final question to ask:

> "How do I compare to other agents you've done business with in the past?"

If it sounds like you are fishing for a compliment, you are. But it's going to be a well-deserved one, and one that has another purpose. You just spent a lot of time and effort discussing their lives and assets, more time than any other agent has ever spent with them.

You are certain to get that compliment, but its purpose isn't to feed your ego. You want clients to say how valuable, trustworthy, and knowledgeable you are because as soon as they put that out into the universe, it reassures *them* that it's true.

A bridge of trust will be forged—and that's a beautiful thing.

7. Show Your Appreciation

This seems obvious, but it's important enough to state clearly: at the end of the annual review, thank them for their business. Some people pay it lip service with a quick, "Thanks, have a good day."

That is never enough. Make your clients understand just how much you appreciate their trust in you. They are allowing you to provide security and protection to them and their family, and that's no small thing.

Showing sincere appreciation will go a long way toward retaining your clients. We send thank you cards to every new business client. It's not just for people who are new to the agency; we also send cards to existing clients who purchase additional policies.

People know the difference between a polite but obligatory thank you and *sincere appreciation*. Be sure your clients know how much you truly appreciate them.

‖‖‖

People want to work with people they like—and being likable gets easier when clients know you have their back. Your agency may represent a large corporation, but once a new client comes aboard, it is your personal agency, and not the faceless organization, that now represents your clients.

If a customer has a bad claim or a negative experience with customer service, *you* want to know about it. If you don't know a problem exists, you can't fix it. The annual review process opens up those lines of communication and fosters a sense of teamwork and cohesiveness that is all too rare these days.

Statistics show that most customers who leave a business wouldn't say they are "dissatisfied." More often than not, people leave because the service they receive is just… forgettable.

So be unforgettable!

Unforgettable service—including an above-and-beyond annual review process—will strengthen relationships, increase retention, and accelerate revenue growth.

Become a
One-Stop Shop

How often have you missed an opportunity to let a client know about all of the services you have to offer and later found out they bought elsewhere? Those painful moments with clients sound something like, "Oh, you needed that? I guess you didn't know we actually offer that here."

So much business slipped through our fingers during the first few years in our agencies. Just the thought of it makes us cringe.

Should you lay it all out for new customers and let them know everything you have to offer at the first meeting? You *could* do that—but we have found that the best time to do this is only after you have established something incredibly important.

That you can be trusted.

Value-added, personalized advice from Trusted Advisors is what drives accelerated growth and revenue. When you and your staff create bonds of trust, customers will allow you to better serve them and will eventually buy multiple policies.

It all comes down to how you train your staff. Are they trusted sources of valuable information or just sales reps? Do they embrace issues or pawn them off to a toll-free number?

Trusted Advisors are counselors. They can sit down with potential clients and provide them with the guidance they need to better meet their family's insurance needs.

Encourage your staff to take on more of a consultant-type role that will foster relationships with your clients that are based on trust, knowledge, and sound advice. After you spend time nurturing those types of connections, cross selling and upselling become the natural next steps in the process. Otherwise, these steps tend to get crammed at the end of a sales presentation and usually come across as awkward, pushy "tactics."

CREATING LIFELONG CUSTOMERS

What can you offer clients that they don't already have? If you have taken the time to get to know them, what they do, and what their priorities are, the answer is a lot!

If you don't ask, you don't know. It's our *duty* to discuss our clients' insurance policies with them. It's also our duty to uncover their passions and priorities in life. Such discussions often lead to the realization that they need even more protection than they thought for the things that matter most. This process allows us get to know our clients, builds trust, and prevents agents from having to say the dreaded words, "Oh, you got that policy somewhere else?"

Spare yourself those cringe-worthy moments and never miss out on opportunities to boost revenue.

To show you just how powerful multi-line customers are, let's look at the retention statistics within our own agencies:

TYPE OF POLICY	RETENTION RATE
Mono-line (single line)	70–75%
Multi-line (two or more policies)	85–90%
Multi-line with an umbrella	95+%

A 95 percent retention rate is unheard of in our industry—but that is the power of the umbrella. When we first started selling umbrella policies, we had heard they were game changers, but we were skeptical. Other agency owners talked about how great they were, but we had yet to see for ourselves. It didn't take long to understand that umbrella policies are potent loyalty instruments that create lifelong clients.

Today, our agents use a waiver form for umbrella policies to ensure that all customers are offered the umbrella. We copied what other successful agency owners were doing, and it helped our agencies sell more umbrella policies, gain higher retention scores, and grow revenue.

You don't have to reinvent the wheel. In fact, it pays to recognize the value of listening to other agents who are doing things right and then putting those winning actions into practice.

THE SKY'S THE LIMIT

If you want to experience explosive growth through new business and customer retention, you should be writing multi-line policies at every opportunity.

And don't forget financial services. According to *Time* magazine, one in every three Americans has saved no money for retirement. That means a large percentage of your customers have no plan for the future.

Will they have enough to last them for the rest of their lives? Will they be able to retire at all?

These questions are weighing on the minds of your customers, and you are in the perfect position, as their Trusted Advisor, to help them figure out the answers.

Offering financial services in addition to insurance products is a natural fit for our agencies. And the benefits are enormous. When we add a financial product into a multi-line household, the retention rate for that group of customers is almost 100 percent!

> **ASA TIP**
>
> As the second most important professionals in our customers' lives, we can't back up that claim if we don't help them plan for their future in every way we can.

Too many people are under-insured and unable to save for retirement—and that's scary. We must make sure our customers know we can lessen the burden of worry about their future by offering the right coverage and the right financial planning help (for agencies who offer such services).

If you don't currently offer financial services, you should consider adding them to your agency's list of capabilities. Provide an invaluable service to your clients, and it will boost your retention to new and greater heights.

Stay in Constant Contact

Annual reviews are, by definition, performed once a year. Is that all the personal contact it takes to improve retention? Um, no.

People are fickle. They have short memories. If you want to keep customers with you, you have to maintain what marketers call TOMA, or *top-of-mind awareness* with them in between reviews.

We've heard agency owners say, "Well, I add every new customer to our email database."

Great! What are you doing with those emails? How are you staying in their conscious space and not slipping into the back of their minds beside the guy who sold them their refrigerator a few years ago?

You must stay in constant contact with customers—and there are many ways you can do this, all of which will foster retention and bring more revenue into your business.

CREATE A MONTHLY NEWSLETTER

If you only communicated with your best friend once a year, would that person really be your best friend? Every relationship needs effort if you want to maintain and develop it.

Given the hectic pace of life today, it's hard to stay in touch with everyone in our lives. Luckily, we have a "life hack" for you that makes maintaining TOMA with your customers so much easier—and it's as simple as a newsletter.

Every month, our agencies send out newsletters or e-magazines to our clients. You may also choose to snail mail the newsletter to your best clients (those with multi-lines and umbrella policies, for example). Our newsletters include things such as recipes, upcoming events in the area, news about some of our clients' businesses, and other useful nuggets of information.

The newsletter allows your clients to stay in the loop about what's going on in your agency and around the community; you can post the winners in your monthly referral program; you can include profiles of your new agents; you can thank all the people who gave you referrals.

If you've been in this field for any length of time, you've heard the idea of sending a monthly newsletter. It's one of those things people say, "Oh yeah, I've thought of that." But are you sending one? Stop thinking about it and start doing it!

The simple act of sending a newsletter will help you stand out among other agencies. It's a way to connect with people and stay top of mind. And just by spending a few hours a month putting together content and blasting it out to customers, you will add twelve more touches per year to every client.

DON'T FORGET THEIR BIRTHDAY

People love birthdays. Even as adults, most of us still get a little excited when someone acknowledges our special day. That is why we instituted a policy of calling our clients on their birthdays.

This is not a call to ask for business. This is not a call to ask for money or a referral. We are not asking them for anything. We simply call to say, "Today is your day. Have an awesome birthday! Thank you for being our client, and if you ever need anything let us know."

We also send birthday cards to customers' children. Adults may not care as much about their birthdays as they age, but both the kids and their parents get a kick out of you remembering a little one's birthday.

These extra-mile actions are actually a lot of fun—you get to step away from your normal duties and bring joy into people's lives. You can make a person's day and have a genuine impact on the lives of others in a personal and meaningful way.

People remember these above-and-beyond gestures, because no one goes above and beyond anymore. Most calls will take less than five minutes but will leave a lasting impact! It's more than worth the minor commitment.

Some people will remember what you say.

A lot of people will remember what you do.

Everyone will remember how you make them feel.

When you call with no agenda other than to simply say "Happy Birthday," it makes a huge impact. They see you as a person, not just some corporation trying to take their money.

START A REFERRAL PROGRAM

When someone agrees to do business with you, that's a big compliment. They trusted you enough to give you money in exchange for protecting the things they care about the most.

When someone gives you a referral, it's an even bigger compliment. They went out on a limb by allowing you to use their good name to market your products and services. Giving you the names of friends, family, neighbors, and co-workers who may be interested in talking with you is no small act. It's an act of trust that should be acknowledged and rewarded.

Asking for referrals should be a part of your annual review process, but you should also be asking for referrals year-round. Starting a referral program is a great way to keep leads coming in all year long and provides another touchpoint to help you stay top of mind with your customers.

The main point of a referral program is to incentivize customers for providing you with names. For example, for every referral they provide, you will donate $10 on their behalf to a special cause. Notice how this act is now about helping someone besides you?

Make sure you keep the referral source (your customer) in the loop. Did the referral agree to meet with you? Become a customer? Let those who gave you referrals know what happened—this is a courtesy and a show of respect, and it also provides you with a reason to reach out to them again. The more touchpoints the better!

BECOME A CONTACT IN THEIR PHONE

Another useful retention "hack" is to ask clients to put your agency's phone number into their phone. The benefit is two-fold: 1) It makes you feel more accessible, and 2) If someone has a referral they want to send your way, it's easier to pass it along. All they have to do is share your contact card from their phone or press a button to reach you.

They no longer have to Google your agency or dig around in their car for your lost business card. Get your phone number programmed into every client's phone, and they can reach you quickly and easily for any reason.

Here's another little-known but great tip for building retention:

Become a contact in their emergency contact's phone.

We ask every client for the name and number of an emergency contact who lives outside of their household—someone who would know if our client didn't show up for work because of an accident, or who could call and start the claims process if our client's house burned down while they were out of town.

Once a new customer joins our agency, we call their contact and introduce ourselves as the client's (their friend's) agent. We let them know that this person selected and trusted them as an emergency contact, and in the event that something happens to their friend or family member, they know to call us first.

We're willing to bet that the emergency contact's insurance agent didn't call *their* emergency contacts—and they will not overlook that fact. Now your phone number is in their phone, and if things go wrong, you are the first person everyone is going to call.

It plants the seed for an indirect referral, and it also fosters retention. Your clients feel safe and secure with an agent who will be willing to go above and beyond to make sure that any problem they have will be dealt with immediately.

NO-AGENDA COMMUNICATION

One of the most important reasons to contact your clients is when you have no reason at all. This is something most agents never do. The industry norm is to maintain radio silence unless there is a problem or a claim. In other words, we only call with bad news, or we are the ones receiving a call from our clients when something bad happens.

In our agencies, we built a system that helps customers stay better connected with us. Every two weeks, we send clients an email that has nothing to do with business. It could be motivational or inspirational; it could be about events in our local community or client appreciation events; it might be helpful tips; it may just serve to keep them informed about the latest news in the agency.

Our goal is to stay connected with customers so that when an insurance need arises, they say, "Hey, I know my insurance agent! He's the one who sends me those emails."

By sending a bi-weekly email, you add 26 touchpoints to the year—and that doesn't count the birthday wishes, monthly newsletter, annual review, and referral calls.

Your customers regularly experience insurance-related events in their lives—shopping for a new car, welcoming a new baby, dealing with the aftermath of a flood or car accident, or buying a new home.

When insurance decisions arise out of those events, who comes to mind?

If you start reaching out to them as much as we do in our agencies, we can guarantee they will be calling *you*.

Even when another provider approaches them and says, "Would you like a quote? I can save you a little money every month," they'll politely decline because the value of staying with you far outweighs any small savings they would gain by switching.

They feel connected with you—and we meet very few customers willing to sacrifice that connection to save a few bucks.

Retention is heavily influenced by how frequently you communicate with your customer base, and that is the big advantage we have as local insurance agents. You are competing against big companies who have the advantage of fancy websites and 800 numbers.

> ## ASA TIP
>
> As small agency owners, we live in the same community as our customers. Take advantage of this proximity and foster genuine relationships with customers.

That's no advantage at all.

We are local. We have faces.

And we build lifelong relationships.

If your customers have an insurance need or question, they can call you—not an automated system that makes them jump through hoops just to talk to a human.

If you want to increase the amount of money coming into your agency, then you have to increase your retention. Regular communication with your customer base will naturally increase retention and grow your reputation as a Trusted Advisor in the community.

Respect the
Other Retention Rate

Every element of retention and revenue growth we've discussed so far is important. But, if we had to pick the one tool you have in your arsenal that trumps all other tools, it's an easy choice.

The most powerful weapon you have is *your human capital*, the men and women you have chosen to surround yourself with every single day.

Your team is your most powerful retention tool—hiring the right team, training the right team, and creating the right environment are the three activities that have the most influence on how effectively you will retain your clients.

If you want your staff to say and do the things that will increase retention, adopt a mentality of "always be learning" in your office. No one is ever through with training. Remember, training is not a single event. Your training process should be its own powerful life force in the office.

Train and role play with your staff daily to ensure they are doing the right activity to find new clients, and even more importantly, doing the right activity to keep the ones your agency already has.

Practice, practice, practice.

In this final chapter on revenue, we will discuss key ways to utilize your biggest asset to grow the bottom line of your business in a mutually beneficial and sustainable way.

TAKE CARE OF YOUR STAFF

We've clearly established the importance of client retention. There is another retention rate that can deeply affect your agency—and that is staff retention.

Maintaining staff stability is critical. When customers join your agency, they are doing so largely because of the agent who sold them their policy. If your agency is a revolving door for agents, you can and will lose credibility with clients. If they have to talk to a different agent every time they call, your agency will certainly lose much of its professional appeal.

We recommend that you pay your staff well, even in the beginning when you don't think you can afford it. If you wait to pay staff well only once you can afford it, you will never be able to afford it, plain and simple.

It's essential that clients view you with a high level of importance, but it's even more essential for your staff to believe and understand their significance. It's up to you to instill in your team the belief that:

- They are Trusted Advisors.
- Their work is important and valuable.
- They are the second most important professionals in their clients' lives.

When you instill these beliefs in your team, they will pass those same attitudes along to their clients.

Your staff needs to believe that what they do impacts lives on a daily basis. Without this level of dedication, your agency's promises of "unparalleled service" will always ring hollow.

Take care of your employees, treat them with respect, and give them the training they need—and they will take care of your clients.

INCENTIVIZE, INCENTIVIZE, INCENTIVIZE

The most important way to increase employee retention is to compensate employees fairly and generously. If your staff feel they are being fairly compensated for the amount of work performed, they will stay with you.

When staff members stay, your business keeps the money it would have had to spend to find, hire, and train new employees. These are real expenses that can be minimized by hiring the right people, providing ongoing training, and paying them according to what they are worth.

Our pay plans are simple. We pay our staff based on their value to the company. We also use a lot of different incentives throughout the year based on overall results.

Pay plans must incentivize producers to want to sell more. For customer service representatives, the pay they receive must be enough to ensure that all clients receive quality care. If you pay minimum wage, you will get minimum-wage work.

In our agencies, a commission-based pay plan works best for sales agents. Although it can be tempting to offer a base pay plus smaller commissions in the short-term, we've found that without a larger commission, salespeople lack the incentive to push for greatness.

How motivated can someone be to write policies if they are only paid a small percentage of the premium? They may give up on prospective clients who would have otherwise signed, because what's the point? It wouldn't make much difference in their paycheck anyway. This type of thinking hurts your revenue, but the clients are the ones who really lose.

Great salespeople want to be rewarded for their efforts. If one producer writes two times as much as the next person, that top performer rightly expects to get paid significantly more than his co-worker.

Salespeople are motivated by competition, the excitement of a sale, and other factors. In the end, however, money is the ultimate motivator.

Think about one of your new agents after she had her first great day: Would you want to pat her on the back and say, "Great job! You earned $90 today." Or would you like to say, "That was unbelievable! Do you realize you just made $360 in one day?"

When you reward her appropriately for a job well done, she will go home feeling confident and excited. When she returns to work the next day, she'll be ready to bring it on again.

The most mutually beneficial way to care for employees is to pay them for doing the right activities, above and beyond their formal commission structure. For example, pay bonuses for renewals. When you do that, your team becomes connected to keeping the business on the books because it affects how they get paid. If they can make money in the form of residual income, they will make sure they lose as few policies as possible!

Taking care of every person in your agency with a solid pay plan is just a smart business move. Evaluate your current compensation plans, and then ask yourself whether you are willing to pay to be surrounded by the best.

PARTICIPATE AS A TEAM IN EVENTS

We love to volunteer and give back to the community. We make our clients aware of the events we plan and the ones in which we actively participate. They also know about the money we raise for charity through our referral programs.

Having a strong positive presence in your community will empower your clients to see you as more than just an insurance agent. It humanizes you and helps others connect with you on a deeper level. Giving back also earns you the respect of your staff and inspires them to stand shoulder to shoulder with you to give back as well.

Consider volunteering in the community at least once a month. Also consider hosting an event or raising money for people with urgent and vital needs in your local community.

Put yourself out front as someone who cares for more than just their insurance agency or themselves. It's important to give back—for your agency, for the community, and for you!

FIND YOUR REVENUE FOCUS

The inability to properly manage revenue will bury any agency. If you are running your agency without a set budget that you observe, there is no doubt your net revenue is suffering. Maybe you are overstaffed. You might be spending too much on marketing. Or you may look at the expenses every month and scratch your head thinking, "Where did all the money go?"

Don't throw money at your agency thinking that one day, this haphazard approach will magically get you where you want to be. The lack of diligent planning and budgeting will result in a whirlwind of random activity with no tangible results.

On the other side of the coin, don't be afraid to invest in the right things. You must have balance to be successful. Be concerned about where your money goes, but also be willing to take risks.

If you invest your money appropriately and wisely, you *will* get a solid return.

Many of the agency owners we know who are resistant to investing in their agency will gladly invest in stocks and mutual funds. They're investing in companies over which they have no control, but they're afraid to invest in their own business!

That makes no sense!

Invest in what you can control. Look at the returns you can get in your own business, simply by growing at a rate of 10 percent a year. Over time, that revenue stream, along with the equity you build, will be tremendous.

Study your gross revenue and net revenue side by side and examine the things that impact both. Make judicious, mindful decisions. Don't be afraid to invest.

And *always* pay attention to your retention rates.

We're in this business to make money. Being smart about your revenue is an important step in making sure more money comes your way, and then keeps coming.

The absolute best way to increase your revenue is to find high-revenue agencies and ask them how they did it. Follow their advice and use it to produce more revenue than you can imagine.

Then someday, you'll be the one giving the advice.

OPERATIONS

Create a System
for Everything

The idea of owning your own business is the true American Dream, isn't it? Be your own boss. Make your own hours. Go on vacation on your terms. Hire whomever you want. Make all the money your family needs.

You can do it your way.

Why, then, do so many entrepreneurs work insane hours and yet seem to be constantly treading water, with their heads barely above the surface?

And why does the reality of achieving this American Dream often seem more like a nightmare for small-business owners?

Starting and growing a business is exciting. It's what entrepreneurs like us thrive on. Yet so often things get out of control. Balls get dropped, and what was once fun and exciting becomes a chore.

After a few months or years of disappointing results, many owners start questioning themselves and wondering what possessed them to start their own agency. Their goals were once freedom, wealth, and independence—now they just feel stuck.

Many throw in the towel at that point and chalk it up as one colossal mistake. They let their dreams die as they trudge back to the nameless, faceless, 9-to-5 workforce.

Sadly, this is how many agency owners' stories end.

This is also what we are trying to prevent.

We've all felt that dream start to fade in the beginning, after the reality sets in of the long hours, unreliable employees, and the general chaos of running a business. Fighting past that chaos is, in fact, the hardest part of what we do.

Nothing makes that chaos more unbearable than operating without a clear set of systems and processes in place. If you do not have distinct processes to follow, you are allowing your entire staff to create and follow their own—and *that* is what leads to the death of the dream.

There can only be one captain of the ship. *You* are the one who sets the course. Once you set the course, you must rely on your crew to navigate you safely to your destination. You can trust your crew—as long as you've given them the right map to get you there.

Are you providing your employees with that map?

You don't want to run an autocracy—you want to operate within a democracy. And the principal feature of a well-run democracy can be summed up with one word: systems.

Without systems, you don't run a business—you *are* the business.

A BIG MAC IS ALWAYS A BIG MAC

One definition of the word *operations* is the "performance of a practical work or of something involving the practical application of principles or processes."[5] This is pretty accurate; a good agency operation is built on the practical application of the right processes. But we've taken the definition a step further:

Operations [noun]:
A collection of systems put in place to *automate daily processes*
that leads to selling more policies and retaining more clients,
which allow agency owners to experience success
and freedom over their time and resources.

The key phrase in the definition is "automate daily processes." A successful agency is one that operates smoothly with or without you.

Agency operations should look the same every day. At any given time, you can walk into a systematized office and find a well-oiled machine at work. Everything has a place. Everyone has defined tasks. No one is left wondering what to do in a key interaction.

An automated office is what allows you to gain *leverage*—and leverage is the key to accelerating growth and scaling a highly profitable agency.

Here's a great example of the power of a successful automated system. Whether you're in California, West Virginia, Texas, or Alaska, a Big Mac is a Big Mac. McDonald's restaurants produce identical products at tens of thousands of different locations because of a well-defined operation, with processes in place for everything.

The taste of the food and the amount of food sold are also not dependent on the owner being there. We've never seen the owner of a McDonald's working at a McDonald's. Have you?

---

5 https://www.merriam-webster.com/dictionary/operation

Have you ever seen an owner flipping burgers or mopping floors? That's not where the owner's value lies. That's not what a business owner should be doing. Smart owners delegate those things to employees.

Systems allow your business to run smoothly. Only then can you have the time to strategize your agency, pursue new opportunities, and continue to develop fresh ideas. Only then can you deliver valuable service and support to every client, no matter the employee, no matter the day, and no matter whether you, the owner, are even there.

DELEGATE TO DUPLICATE

We mentioned that McDonald's owners never flip the burgers. *Do you think there are ever times when they're tempted to flip the burgers?* Let's say they see a new hire doing it incorrectly. It's easy to assume part of them wants to take over and just "get it done."

We can relate; it's hard to watch people make mistakes and not intervene.

This is the inherent problem with delegating: you have to be able to trust that an employee will eventually do it correctly.

As difficult as that can be, it must be done, because delegation is the first necessary step toward setting up a successful agency operation. You are running a multi-faceted enterprise, not a mall kiosk.

For most leaders we know, delegation is one of their biggest fears. It was ours, too. We used to believe the only way to get things done right was to do them ourselves. That belief was grounded in some truth. If you make desperation hires and operate based on fear, delegation absolutely *can* be a disaster.

Because we hadn't hired right, we ended up making every single decision. That meant if we wanted to double revenue, we needed to double the number of the hours we worked. Since there are only so many hours in a day, that plan put a serious limit on our growth potential.

It's tempting to equate long hours to success—but one of the many problems with 16-hour days is they simply aren't sustainable if you want to have any quality of life.

What it really comes down to is "dollar-per-hour" thinking. Do you think working 60 hours a week will make you successful? How many hours a day can you work before you hit your maximum potential?

As a one-man or one-woman show, you'll eventually find your limit.

Fortunately, there is a solution. *Duplication* is what that takes away all limits and opens the floodgates of potential.

In the beginning, duplication could be as simple as delegating someone to answer the phone. By assigning this task to someone else, you have more time to call prospective clients. Once you hire new agents and train them properly to do their jobs, you have more time to file claims. Once you hire a claims specialist, you have time to focus on hiring more people.

On it goes until eventually, you have duplicated yourself to the point that the business is growing without you.

It takes time and money to reach that level. But even if your book of business is small right now, you still have the ability to do this on some level, until your book generates the kind of cash flow necessary to maintain a larger staff and accomplish a high level of duplication.

Imagine what it would feel like to make exceptional money while you're

> ## ASA TIP
>
> If you're working 60 hours a week, stop spinning your wheels and start thinking about the tasks you do every day that could be delegated to someone else. Duplicate yourself.

on vacation, or to know that you are able to leave a powerful legacy behind for your children.

Hire the right people and set the agency up to succeed through the right systems and delegation, and that can be your future.

WHAT TRANSFORMS AVERAGE INTO EXCEPTIONAL

It would be beyond the scope of this book to lay out in detail every single system you should have in place. The reason is that you need systems for everything! You need them in order to:

- Do performance reviews
- Train your team
- Gather employee feedback
- Motivate your employees
- Pay salaries and commissions
- Call on prospective customers
- Call on existing customers
- Attain and collect feedback from clients
- Notify customers about policy changes
- Do expense and financial planning
- Pay for purchases
- Determine your marketing ROI

You'll also need systems for setting up and using technology; for providing tax documentation and legal contracts; for communicating internally and externally. You'll even need them for simple things such as how to handle lunch times (staggered lunches, length of lunch, etc.).

These are a few examples of many automated processes that should be running in your agency. It can overwhelm even the most seasoned entrepreneur. That is why we have simplified things by placing all processes into four main categories. So far, we have covered: 1) Our proven *Hiring* system, 2) The processes that create and maintain the right *Environment*, and 3) Processes for boosting *Revenue* and retention.

In this final section of the book, we're talking about the fourth part of the H.E.R.O. system, which is *Operations*. We will discuss how to:

- Refine sales operations
- Build your marketing strategy
- Foster the communication process
- Practice specialization
- Systematize accountability

The right processes and systems are the keys to establishing successful operations. They breed agency-wide consistency and excellence, which translate into long-term success for your agency and for you.

Foster a Culture
of Sales Excellence

If we gave agency owners the opportunity to ask us just one question, we know what the majority of them would ask:

"How can we sell more policies?"

The answer is to put the right processes in place for your staff—and that includes setting them up to win through structured sales processes.

You may not be able to change your team's inherent skill level, degree of raw talent, or even what motivates them, but you *can* change how you teach people to do their job. This chapter will highlight the sales processes that consistently achieve explosive results.

Hire right, train right, and trust the process to do the rest.

ASSUME NOTHING

Your new agents have a lot of work they must do before they get hired; they have to pass a rigorous profile test; make it through several rounds of interviews; spend lots of time studying; and pay money to get licensed.

Once they are hired, it's your responsibility to provide them with every opportunity to do their job well. Hiring the right candidate does not guarantee success. You must hand them the tools to succeed.

Your systems and processes are those tools.

In our agencies, we don't assume anyone knows how to sell. We don't assume anyone knows how to connect and build relationships. In fact, we assume nothing.

We don't rely on assumptions or guesswork. We have defined processes that lay out the direction our agents should go at every point in their daily interactions. We teach our people what every touch with customers is supposed to look like—from the initial contact to each communication after the sale.

> ### ASA TIP
>
> If you want your employees to habitually say and do the things you know will lead to more sales and greater retention, then you have to spell out *exactly* what those things are—and then constantly inspect what you expect.

Having a system through which all client interaction flows prevents individual agent bias from clouding a sales situation. Too often, salespeople express themselves based on how they would personally respond or react to a situation. They consider their own current life experiences and assume the client feels the same way, too.

For example, a salesperson who is struggling to pay the bills may recommend the least expensive insurance, because that's what he would choose.

But what if a client wants the best package money can buy? What if a client has the means to pay in full and save even more, but he or she never knew this was possible because the agent didn't present that option? What if that extra savings is what could have closed the deal or kept the client from leaving at renewal time?

Another example of how assumptions can cloud the situation comes in the form of something we all experience daily in this profession: rejection.

Let's say an agent just had three unsuccessful annual reviews where all three customers cancelled their policies. That's deflating, no matter how you spin it. How can you prevent such a big momentum killer from causing an agent to assume that everyone else she talks to that day must also want to cancel their policies?

Employees may use their personal life experiences to unintentionally guide the sales process, even if it may not be best for that client.

But aren't we all biased in some way?

Making assumptions is part of our human nature, right?

It may be human nature to make assumptions based on surface stuff—and sure, we've all done it—but that doesn't mean you can't do it a better way.

You can fight that tendency simply by listening. The most important process you can emphasize is the practice of listening. Teach your team to hear what customers have to say. Then you can provide them with the best advice based on their unique circumstances, rather than on assumptions.

FOLLOW THE PATH

Sales scripts have their place. However, most scripts are ineffective because the majority of people can't or won't internalize them. They memorize the words on the paper that someone else wrote and deliver them like a robot.

Robots may be able to build cars, but they can't sell insurance. People buy from people they like and with whom they feel a connection.

We recommend using *talk paths* in our communications with prospective customers and clients. Talk paths are less like word-for-word scripts and more like roadmaps.

To show you how talk paths work, let's consider the process of quoting a prospect. Ideally, you want all employees to quote everyone in the same way. Uniformity prevents agents from skipping vital information. Talk paths answer important questions, such as:

- What key points must be included in every sale?
- How do agents go about covering these points?
- At what point in the interaction should agents quote prospects?
- What should agents say when they do give the quote?
- And much, much more.

Ideally, everyone in your agency should approach communication with clients in the same manner. Talk paths provide them with a proven way to deal with the most common scenarios they will encounter.

For your free copy of a sample talk path you can use to guide your agents down the right road, visit: agencysalesacademy.com/growth.

BUILD BRIDGES, NOT ROADBLOCKS

A multitude of things can derail agents from the path—interruptions, objections, and a long list of distractions. As part of our sales process, we teach agents how to carefully address and overcome common roadblocks in order to stay on the road to a successful close.

How many times have you spoken with a prospect who's in a hurry? Instead of leaving responses to chance, coach your team on how to handle the "I'm in a big hurry" objection *before* it comes up. Be proactive!

Teach them to reassure the client:

"I understand your time is valuable, Mrs. Client, so let's not waste any of your time and get this done for you right away. Sound good? Now, what is your address, so we can get moving…"

When a client feels that you respect her time, she can start to relax. Acknowledge the client's concern by letting her know you heard what she said. Of course, we know that a talk path is designed to be respectful of a client's time. So, once you have reassured the client, you'll jump right back onto the designated path that leads to the quote.

What you want to avoid are statements like, "I understand, Mrs. Client; just give me two more minutes of your time to collect the data I need to start a quote."

This response not only sounds desperate, but it also does nothing to build that vital bridge between you and your client. In fact, you are letting her know this is a very *transactional* conversation.

We deal with people, not transactions. Teach your team to respond to common

> ## ASA TIP
>
> We don't like the word *transaction*. These are *people*, not search engines. Our job is to build relationships with clients, because clients want to do business with people they know, like, and trust!

objections in a way that says to the client, "This agent understands me and my needs, so it must be worth my time."

INSTILL A CULTURE OF LISTENING

How many social settings have you been in where insurance is the talk of the party? It never happens. Ever. People want to talk about four basic things: family, occupation, recreation, or motivation—that's it.

Also, if given the choice, people would much rather talk about themselves. It's just the way we are wired.

Here is the big takeaway. There is a time and a place to get into the details of a policy, but that time can only come *after* you have established the fact that you are in the business of helping people protect what they care about, not the business of successfully completing a sale.

That is why we encourage client conversations to center on *anything* other than insurance.

Find out what's most important to them. Some people love their family; some can't stand their family. Others love their job and enjoy talking about what they do.

Teach your team to avoid the urge to pigeonhole based on assumptions. Instead, they must consciously and actively look for ways to connect by asking questions. If you slow down and listen, clients will present you with ways to build that necessary bridge of connection.

Our process teaches entry points of conversation that can lead to building a better relationship with our clients. For example:

Connect Through Location. When a client provides his address, say, "Hmm, that sounds familiar. Where exactly is that?" Once he clarifies, come up with a connection. Maybe it's a restaurant in the neighborhood; maybe your uncle lives nearby; maybe your kids go to the same school. Take a few extra seconds to uncover a connection point.

Connect Through Hobbies. Another area that provides you with opportunities to connect is hobbies. If you have a real interest in classic cars, and a customer owns a 1957 Chevy, ask a few questions or show your own knowledge of the subject.

Connect Through Pets. Do you hear a dog barking in the background on a phone call with a client? People love talking about their pets! Ask about Fido; get people talking about their fuzzy friends, and if you have any pets of your own, let them know.

Connect Through Unique Features. If you notice a client is wearing something unusual such as a big hat or large belt buckle, you could say, "Wow, what a great hat. Where did you get that?" This person obviously wants it to be noticed, and we have found that unique pieces usually have a great story behind them.

Connect Through Passions. The hardest thing to uncover (but the best way to connect) is to focus on what really motivates clients. What is their passion? When you figure this out and show genuine interest, it creates a strong and powerful bond.

We want to be very clear—the goal is not to pretend to share a common interest or say whatever it takes to make the sale. This process simply allows for open conversations that will enable you to connect as you uncover opportunities. This is a necessary step in becoming a Trusted Advisor.

Get to know your clients! The importance of this process cannot be overemphasized. When we walk through our agencies, we want to hear fewer coverage discussions and more conversations about what inspires and motivates our clients.

INVITE EMOTION TO THE PARTY

Despite the fact that the public thinks what we do is static and boring —and it can be monotonous, like any other career—our job is actually filled with emotion.

When a person gets into a car accident, there is so much at stake. No doubt it was terrifying. There could have been serious injuries, or worse. What if there were children involved?

As you sit in front of perfectly healthy prospects, it can be difficult to imagine this end of our business—but it's there. It's the reason we are in business in the first place.

Your agents should be conveying the emotion of what "protection" really means to prospective clients. If they are not already doing this, they are missing a huge opportunity to connect and to transform the common perceptions of salespeople.

We are insurance agents, not statisticians—and more important than reciting the details of every policy or giving prospects a rundown of insurance stats, you must convey the emotion behind the policy.

We unquestionably include discussion about coverage on our talk paths, but we focus more on the *why* behind the coverage, or what each type of coverage means to customers.

Give real examples that are relatable and convey emotion. Tell the story about the client who got sued after she accidentally struck a pedestrian who darted across the street into oncoming traffic. Without proper liability coverage, she would have had a huge financial burden that would have adversely affected the rest of her life and her children's lives. Fortunately, she was covered properly.

Whenever we relate a true story, it becomes real to the client, and it turns the policy into something more than just another monthly expense. It also allows us to more naturally lead into a conversation about opting for extra liability, above and beyond what other carriers usually provide.

This is also an opportunity to discuss standard collision versus broad coverage. We always recommend broad coverage, since it provides full coverage with no deductible as long as they are not at fault in the accident. We tell them that we don't feel they should be penalized if they were not at fault, then (as part of the process) we tell a true story about a not-at-fault accident and how difficult such an expense can be.

Using a *qualified coverage form* is another process we have in place in our agencies. The qualified coverage form lists all of the coverages we offer. Our agents go through the form with clients, and after they've said yes or no to each piece, we have them sign it. It is an upsell tool that lets them know everything they qualify or don't qualify for, but it's also an educational tool. People don't know what they don't know. Help them learn what true protection really looks like and how they can protect every area of their lives.

To download a free sample of the type of qualified coverage form we use in our agencies, please visit: agencysalesacademy.com/growth.

TRACK PRODUCTION

Finally, as a part of the sales process, we send emails to all staff about the day's productivity. If someone writes a policy, everyone knows about it immediately. The email includes which agent is responsible for the business and the type of policy or policies sold. These messages serve to acknowledge and appreciate each success, and they act as motivational tools by sparking healthy competition.

Our sales process also includes doing a daily rundown of all team activity with the sales managers at the end of the day. We discuss each agent's activity, and plan for the following day. Each morning, our sales managers will meet with the staff to recap the previous day, review the action plan for the new day, and then continue to train and role play.

Doing this consistently holds everyone on the team accountable. Review results daily so that your staff knows you are *always inspecting what you expect.*

Without sales, you don't have an agency. Don't leave their success up to chance—provide agents with every tool they need to get the job done.

Learn the Process for Finding New Customers

Great agents ask smart questions in order to connect and uncover needs. They know how to close a deal. They have outstanding follow-up systems. They have great attitudes, and they encourage others in the office to do their best.

However, a salesperson without prospects is as useful as a doctor without patients. That's why the one trait our most successful agents have in common more than any other is that they view prospecting as a top priority.

They see opportunities everywhere, and they know it's not just a numbers game—but the numbers still matter.

Provide your team with a prospecting plan. Before they ever make their first call, they need to feel confident in the process and know they are calling on qualified prospects.

Without a prospecting plan, your agents will waste valuable time and energy calling on dead leads. After a few months of frantic "smiling and dialing" with no plan in place, even the most optimistic agent will lose confidence and eventually quit.

DEFINE THE PROSPECTING PROCESS

If all you have is a name, you have only the possibility of developing a prospect. The diagram below shows the process of moving a name from a lead to a qualified prospect.

It's so simple and yet so hard. You have to answer questions like these for your staff before they even come up:

- Where do new leads come from?
- How do we qualify leads?
- Will we know who to call, how to reach them, and what to say?
- What kind of ongoing training can we expect?

Top-performing agencies clearly define the prospecting process and help their agents find who to call. Agency owners and sales managers define the process, consistently teach it, and inspect what they expect.

Giving agents directives like "quote ten prospects a day" is useless as a call to action. That's a great goal, but it doesn't tell them how to go about accomplishing it.

Goals with no action plan are pointless. Set your team up to succeed by providing them with a system that brings in new prospects and keeps their pipelines robust. Of course, this plan leads to even more questions, such as:

- What lists should we be using?
- How do we know which leads are viable on this list?
- What do we say once we actually have someone on the line?

Finding new prospects is a challenge for every agency. But, if you've ever tried to prospect without a plan in place, you know there is almost no greater motivation killer. There are few things as disheartening as going through the entire sales process only to discover that the person you spent 45 minutes speaking with was never even a qualified prospect.

Your sales staff may have all the right qualifications on paper. They may look like natural born salespeople on their personality profiles. But if they get stuck

> ## ASA TIP
>
> ||||||||||||||||||||||||||||||||||||||||||||||||||||
>
> Mix up your lists and prospecting techniques. Salespeople get bored and frustrated when they have to do the same thing every day. Encourage them to find their own referral sources, and continually teach effective prospecting skills.

in the muck and mire of prospecting, none of that will matter. They'll get frustrated, make mediocre money, and eventually quit or be fired.

Whatever process has worked for you in the past, write it out and pass it on to your staff. Help them avoid some of the worst prospecting pitfalls and keep their momentum.

MAKE GETTING REFERRALS A DAILY ACTIVITY

When should your agents ask for referrals? Only on the days they want to make more money. Referrals are a key ingredient in the accelerated growth formula. They take cold calls and turn them into warm calls that lead to new policies faster than any other method of prospecting.

There are two main reasons customers do not immediately provide referrals. First, they find it difficult to think of names. The second reason is they consider themselves *conscientious objectors*—they do not want to give referrals because they don't want co-workers, friends, or family to feel pressured into buying something.

We have found about 20 percent of clients won't give referrals no matter how you ask. Another 20 percent will easily and happily offer them. It's the other 60 percent where a plan of action is essential.

Your agents don't get more referrals because they don't ask for them, so it's time to teach them how to ask.

What to Ask. You are looking for the names and preferred method of contact for people your clients consider to be potential candidates for your products. Since we have yet to meet a person who doesn't need some form of insurance, it's hard to imagine a client not knowing at least one person who could benefit from what you have to offer. The variable in each situation is how this contact should be made.

What to ask for depends on your customer's need for control of the situation. Here is what we mean:

- Some customers want to handle communication themselves. This is rare but it happens.
- Others want minimal involvement. They prefer that you initiate the contact for them, but they will want to know how it goes.
- You may come across some customers who have specific instructions regarding what they want you to do or say with their referrals. Giving you names of their friends and colleagues is a big deal to them, and they want to make sure they can trust you with this responsibility.

The best way to find out how much control your client wants to have is to ask: "Do you prefer me to call Mr. Referral and report back to you, or do you want to initiate the introduction?"

Whatever prospecting and referral systems you choose, make all activity available to everyone in the office. Correspondence with potential clients and existing clients must be entered into your shared CRM system. This prevents agents from unintentionally poaching leads and makes everyone's activities more streamlined.

DISCOVER AFFORDABLE MARKETING METHODS

Marketing is an interesting topic in the world of insurance. Some great agencies spend very little on marketing; some invest a lot of time, money, and effort in the hopes that qualified prospects will call them, rather than the other way around.

Whatever your marketing approach, here are a few no-cost strategies to consider:

Work the No's. One incredible and often overlooked source of new customers is to circle back to the no's you hear every day from people who decline your products.

It's helpful to adopt the mentality that they don't really mean *no*—they just mean "not right now." If you had a great call with a prospect who decided not to become a customer, there is no reason to assume he will not eventually become a customer when the time is right. Do what it takes to stay top of mind with "not right now" prospects through newsletters and emails. If you provide useful information to them throughout the year, you can feel totally justified in checking in with them again at their renewal time.

If you continue to follow up in a professional and helpful manner with these prospects and consistently build your value as a Trusted Advisor, there's a good chance they will eventually become clients.

Start a Renter's Program. Introducing yourself to renters in apartment complexes is a smart way to add prospects to the pool. Many of those renters will eventually become homeowners. Make the rounds every month, and you'll always see new faces; there's a lot of turnover in that market. It's also a good idea to build relationships with new apartment employees. You never know who might send business your way.

A renter's program is a creative way to get leads for auto policies and to build a respectable homeowners' book of business. If you're not offering renter's insurance because those policies don't stay on the books, you may want to reconsider. If you stay top of mind with these customers, your name will be the one they remember when the time is right.

Check Your ROI. There is no one-size-fits-all marketing system. Really, the only limits to how you market are your levels of creativity, ingenuity, and drive. Whatever marketing choices you make, consistently follow up on your efforts to determine your return on investment. If something isn't bringing in enough revenue to justify the time or expense, scrap it and find another way.

IMPLEMENT A CONCIERGE PROGRAM

As insurance agents, we sell intangible products. We decided to support those products with a more tangible service known as a "concierge program." Like the concierge services at a luxury hotel, our programs strive to make life easier for clients and add tremendous value in more ways than just the protection our policies provide.

Once a person becomes a client, they have immediate access to a list of services and discounts they can't get anywhere else. Common services offered include:

1. Discounts on tickets for plays, concerts, and sporting events
2. Exclusive offers on travel and vacations
3. Deals on transportation services and restaurants
4. Special offers on home and car maintenance services such as plumbing, landscaping, house cleaning, and auto repair
5. Relocation services and affordable pet care
6. Unique deals on gifts, flowers, and hard-to-find items

Starting your own concierge program can be simple. No doubt you already have clients on the books who can offer discounted, valuable services to other clients, and would be more than happy to do so. Take a look at your existing customer base and see who might be interested in a partnership. You'll be benefiting both their business and yours, so there really is no downside.

DEFINE YOUR ONLINE PRESENCE

A strong online presence is another essential way to gain new business and maintain a strong connection within your agency's community. We train our agents to go through our websites and social media pages with new clients. We want customers to know what features are available on our site and how to find out more about our referral and concierge programs.

The point is to make it as easy as possible for them to find helpful, interesting, and useful information. Make your newsletter available on your site, and update your social media pages frequently to give people a reason to keep checking back in with your agency.

The bottom line is that with dozens or even hundreds of other agencies just within your city limits that can provide similar products, why should anyone choose you?

What can you offer that others cannot?

What makes you different?

Once you determine how and why you are different, publicize those differentiating competitive advantages as part of your daily and monthly operations.

Develop a Culture
of Communication

How much time gets wasted in your office every day?

If most agency owners are honest with themselves, the answer is a lot.

How much wasted time are your employees really spending texting their buddies, forwarding funny emails, Snapchatting, and taking a Facebook quiz to find out which *Star Wars* character they are?

Some polls suggest that people waste as much as ten minutes every hour, and some waste much more. Many of your employees aren't even aware they are time wasters, because so much of this wasted time is involved in unconscious lost minutes.

According to *Entrepreneur Magazine*, employees are wasting time each day in the following areas:[6]

---

6 https://www.entrepreneur.com/article/272379

1. **Rituals.** We all have certain actions we do every day in the office (take long breaks, get coffee, chat near the water cooler, etc.). Some of these are productive and necessary; many are not.

2. **Distractions.** This vast and wide-reaching category includes the most grievous time waster of all—the use of personal technology, including checking personal email and social media accounts, texting, and talking on the phone to friends and family.

3. **Ineffective Communication.** Have you ever spent 30 minutes writing an email when a two-minute phone call would have accomplished the same thing? That is an ineffective use of your time. Meetings and emails, in a perfect world, always add to the bottom line. In the real world, they are notorious time wasters. Make all meetings and emails count. Think before you meet or write. If there is a more efficient way to get it done, find it.

4. **Refusal to Adapt.** Are you stuck in a routine, even when situations change? Refusing to adapt your working style or focus when situations shift will cost you dearly in terms of time spent.

5. **Working on the Wrong Priorities.** What is the fastest way to the cash? If you are not working on things that directly address that question, then you need to readjust your priorities and stop burying yourself in busywork to avoid the real work of growing the business. Talking to new and existing customers is always a good idea. Making sure your email inbox is cleaned out? Not so much.

We have about 20 actual workdays every month. Factor in the amount of time wasted through the actions above, and you probably lose a full two days, leaving you with 18 days, on a good month.

What can you do to make the most out of your limited and valuable time? The answer is to set expectations and define the activities that should be filling the calendars of your staff. Then you have to inspect what you expect.

LIVE AND DIE BY THE CALENDAR

Everyone in the office should be using a shared agency calendar and agency management system. Everything should be on that calendar, and they should operate according to what is on that agenda as if their life depended on it. Here are some guidelines for getting the most out of your office calendar:

1. **Put everything in the calendar.** A calendar system won't keep you organized if you don't put every single aspect of your workday into it. From lunchtime to the time you plan to spend prospecting, account for every hour of your day.

2. **Utilize time blocking.** Time blocking is an effective strategy for achieving greater productivity. First, identify your high priority tasks and projects, and then break tasks down into chunks that can be completed in smaller time increments. Be sure to schedule regular breaks; they are conducive to greater productivity and concentration. Limit activities that interfere with your time blocking goals, and let others know you will be unavailable during certain times.

3. **Use color-coding.** Color coding, especially when it comes to shared calendars, can be helpful. Assign a specific color to use for all new prospect appointments, annual reviews, and so on.

4. **Set recurring dates and reminders.** If you do something over and over again, use your calendar's recurrence feature to automatically set up all future occurrences of that same activity. Then set up reminders that will alert you a few minutes or hours before an event.

5. **Send meeting notices.** Most calendar systems will let you schedule an appointment and then send people an invitation. Use this feature to schedule interviews with potential new hires, remind employees about meetings, and set up phone calls or meetings with new or existing clients.

Whatever calendar system you decide to use, make sure everyone in the office is doing the same thing.

DON'T TOUCH ANYTHING TWICE

Another process that can save you a great deal of time is to observe what we call the "don't touch anything twice" rule. It's a philosophy that gets people thinking about the simplest, most streamlined way to do daily tasks.

Here is an example: Ban the use of pens and paper in your office. Instead, train your staff that every piece of information about a client and every communication should be noted inside your digital management system. If an agent writes information down on a piece of paper, she is going to eventually have to type it out as well—and that's "touching it twice." This takes two times the amount of effort and time, which is inefficient for the agency.

The simplest changes can save you tons of valuable time.

UTILIZE THE BEST TECHNOLOGY

Technology can be a huge time waster. However, the right technology can also become one of the best assets in your agency.

There's a lot to learn about technology when it comes to our business. There are four critical technology components that your office needs to run as efficiently as possible:

1. **ISP.** First, you need a good Internet Service Provider (ISP). The most important aspect is speed. Make sure the Internet, email, and everything else that requires a connection are able to run quickly and without interruption. Never skimp on bandwidth. No matter which provider you choose (Comcast, AT&T, etc.), get the most bandwidth possible.

2. **SIP.** Next, you need a good Session Initiation Protocol (SIP) carrier, which is used for signaling and controlling multimedia communication sessions, such as video calls over Internet Protocol (IP) networks.

3. **VoIP.** You also need a solid Voice over Internet Protocol (VoIP) phone system. VoIP is hardware and software that enables you to use the Internet as the transmission medium for telephone calls. Your VoIP should have certain functionality. It has to have reporting options, recording functions, and the ability to transfer calls easily. It also should be user-friendly; your staff won't be able to use it efficiently if it's cumbersome.

4. **CRM.** Finally, you need a CRM system that is universally accessible and tracks all interactions with clients. A CRM system manages two key things—clients and staff. *Everything* that happens with your clients and staff should be done within your management system. In our offices, if it's not in the system, it didn't happen. With no documentation, it might as well not exist. Make sure your staff understands that everything they do should be entered into that management system.

One other efficient technology idea is to add dual monitors to everyone's workstation. This small addition can make a huge difference. With all the different technologies and tasks to manage throughout the day, one monitor is nowhere near enough. Two monitors will

ASA TIP

||||||||||||||||||||||||||||||||||||||||||||||||||||||||

Technology is not an area of business to sacrifice for the sake of a few dollars. Don't be wasteful; choose options that will help you and your team be as efficient as possible.

do wonders for your efficiency, and it's an inexpensive investment (you can purchase monitors for under $100 apiece).

Investing in efficient technology is an investment in your own success, but keep in mind that technology can *accelerate* momentum; but it doesn't *create* it. You can't create a great business just by adding new technology. However, it can enhance the work of a motivated team already doing the kind of work that leads to results.

A MOTIVATED STAFF IS AN EFFICIENT STAFF

Investing in the efficiency of your agency's system is not all about ISP and bandwidth. It's also essential to find proven, duplicable ways to keep your staff locked in and motivated to sell and represent your agency with their best foot forward. Here is an idea that may work for those who enjoy sports. Break your agent's days into four quarters:

1st Quarter 9–11 A.M.
2nd Quarter 11–1 P.M.
3rd Quarter 1–3 P.M.
4th Quarter 3–5 P.M.

In each quarter, focus their energy on getting first downs, not throwing Hail Mary passes. First downs are sales activities. The numbers that matter are daily actions like the number of quotes given, or financial discussions held. Those key metrics get emailed to you or the sales manager at the end of every quarter to let you know where agents stand hourly, not just daily. If you notice that an agent's numbers are really off for two or more "quarters" in a row, you have the opportunity to step in and coach before the entire day is a loss.

We like to reward each day's winners. Whoever has the most points (quantifiable sales activity, not necessarily sales) can spin a wheel or roll dice for a gift card or the opportunity to leave early on Friday afternoon.

The best agents tend to identify with the competitive nature of athletics, but a sports theme may not work for your office. Whatever motivational theme you choose to use based on the personal preferences and tastes of your staff, make sure it is systematized so that you regularly celebrate both big and small victories in your agency.

KEEP ALL COMMUNICATION UNIFORM

Another often-overlooked agency process is communication. Systematizing the way everyone within your agency communicates with prospects and clients can be a real game changer.

One of the best ways to accomplish this is to have templates for *everything*. When your staff communicates with clients via email, have them use email templates that are already formatted for every foreseeable situation. That way, you communicate with all clients consistently and professionally, not to mention your staff will save a ton of time by no longer having to create emails from scratch.

We also recommend all team members send their correspondence directly from your digital management system. That way emails are attached to each client's file. In the event that someone on your staff leaves, you do not lose communication with that client or have to filter through their old emails.

HAVE AWESOME MEETINGS

Communication is such a vital part of what we do with clients, but as the head of your agency, it's just as vital to communicate with your entire team on a daily basis.

Have daily morning meetings. These meetings should not be spent criticizing or applying unnecessary pressure. They should be used for training and role-playing. The three items on the agenda for your meetings should be:

1. Goal Setting

Set goals, but don't chastise your staff when they are not met. Keep meetings upbeat, no matter how everyone is performing. Use meetings to build up rather than tear down by highlighting who is doing well. Bringing the team together to yell at them for not doing a good job might work for an athletic coach, but in your agency, it will only breed discontent.

In our meetings, we use various ways to motivate our team to reach their full potential. Having contests works well, but only if you take the time to find out what types of rewards work for your employees. Do they like cash? Do they like trips? Time off work? Recognition awards? Once you determine what lights a fire under them, design contests around those things.

2. Accountability

Meetings are a great way to hold everyone accountable for their daily actions, because they always know they will be meeting soon to discuss results.

Beyond daily meetings with the entire office, we meet with our managers weekly to discuss goals and training plans. Our teams set weekly goals every Monday, both personally and professionally. This gives us and our sales managers the opportunity to not only discuss the week's business objectives, but also to get a glimpse into the personal side of each agent.

Personal obstacles often hold team members back from their professional goals. While you can't do much to help them with personal problems (that's not your job and never will be), you can help show them how to separate the professional the personal once they walk through the agency doors.

> **ASA TIP**
>
> We have learned over the years that employees work far better under an air of motivation than one of criticism.

We are all dealing with stuff. Compartmentalizing is a necessary skill if you want to be successful—and the more you can remind them of that, the better.

3. Role Play

Your morning training sessions are the ideal time to engage in role-playing. We highly value the importance of role playing in our agencies. Frankly, we love meetings! They provide us with the opportunity to practice with the team, find out how much our agents have in their pipeline, see what they are working on, and discover where they are encountering roadblocks along the sales path.

By having those daily interactions, you will discover ways to help your team in a significant way.

HAVE AN OPERATIONS MANUAL

An essential, non-negotiable piece of your successful agency system is the "Bible" of your agency, also known as the *operations manual.*

Every agency's operations manual looks different. For some it may be a massive 1,000-page manual that details every procedure.

For others, it may be a series of simple checklists stored in a binder or as an online document. The only requirement is that you have a written plan that you and your employees can reference when they need to know something.

The operations manual should also serve as your agency's training guide. That way, everyone understands all systems and processes, how they work, what's going to be *expected*, what's going to be *inspected*, and how they get paid.

If you don't have an operations manual, start creating one now. Include your hiring and training policies, compensation structure, referral program, concierge program, sales talk paths, checklists for important daily activities, and how-to guides for each system you have in place.

When you find things that work for your agency, write them down and add them to your manual. *It's a living document that should grow and change over time, just like your business.*

What processes do you currently have that may need to be updated? Maybe you do something differently today than your formal process calls for, but your manual does not reflect that.

Get it out, dust it off, and make the change. Your entire team will benefit.

Have a
Social Media Mindset

Social media is a waste of time.

At least that's what a lot of businesspeople think. We all use it to keep up with friends and family. But when it comes to our business, it's just for building brand awareness and doing promotions, right?

Can it really lead to more policies?

Absolutely.

In this chapter, we're going to discuss the basics of how to make social media a critical part of your daily processes in a way that is useful and profitable.

The secret but not-so-secret key to getting the full benefit of social media is to put yourself out there rather than stand behind the curtain of your agency. Tangible leads and meaningful connections happen not through the agency page but mostly through personal interactions with people in your community, with influencers, with existing clients, and with potential customers.

Why would you ever want to "put yourself out there" on social media to people you don't know? That's an easy one to answer:

Social media is your competitive advantage.

There are two billion people on Facebook alone, and if you and your agents are not operating in that space, you are missing a huge opportunity. The advantage online is yours to take, so let's learn how to harness its awesome power.

Social media is limited only by your creativity and your willingness to be bold and authentic. The great news is it's easier than you think to make an impact online.

GIVE CUSTOMERS WHAT THEY REALLY WANT

We know people do business with those they know, like, and trust. In today's increasingly virtual society, social media is the fastest and most efficient way to identify potential customers so they can get to know you, like you, and see you as a Trusted Advisor.

Social media is just one more place to market yourself—and if you have been in business for any period of time, you've learned that we should be marketing our talents, our products, and ourselves constantly.

Our entire lives are spent marketing. It's all about how you present yourself, what connections you make, and what impression you leave with others. Embrace this truth, and you'll begin to see the importance of utilizing social media to let people get to know you, your family, and your business.

You will never be able to amass much of a following if you only post about agency or insurance topics. People want real! People want interesting! People want relatable! People want you to make their lives better—or at least a little easier.

Here's a great example: Say you're about to board a plane and you post a quick live video that starts with, "Hey guys, I am here at the airport, and I would like to share my secrets for getting upgraded to first class…"

This has nothing to do with your business, so why post it? We can think of several reasons: 1) Videos are memorable, 2) Videos allow viewers to feel they are getting to know you, and 3) Giving your followers tips that will legitimately add value to their lives is always a good thing, no matter the topic.

In our line of work, it's not really about how much insurance knowledge we can spit out. It's about connecting on a real level with people. Social media is a platform on which to connect, to be a referral source, to be a person of value, and to sidestep the "just another pushy salesperson" stigma.

DON'T EXPECT NEW RESULTS WITH OLD MARKETING

Plenty of online businesses use social media exclusively to inform the public about discounts or other news about their business. The problem with that is it's *old* marketing. A few years ago, such tactics may have been good enough—but things have evolved way beyond these rudimentary practices.

Your educated potential buyers already know a lot about your product and what they want before they even *start* shopping agencies. However, one fact remains certain forever: they are going to do business with someone they know, like, and trust. When they feel like they already know you because you've let your personality shine online, you increase the odds of being the obvious choice for their insurance needs.

As a bonus, you've potentially shortened the sales cycle by doing some of the trust building virtually. They see your videos. They see your kids win the big game. They comment on your posts. You comment on theirs. This all serves to create bonds—and the result:

Everybody benefits.

When you create a powerful social media presence, people in your community will begin to recognize you on the street! The first time that happens, it's an amazing feeling, because it means that people with whom are engaging online legitimately feel connected to you offline. In the future, when those people need an insurance agent, you *know* they are going to think of you.

ASA TIP

Our goal is to leave people better off—and social media provides us with a way to make people's lives a little better, even if they never become customers.

No one enjoys the feeling of being "sold." That's the beauty of online social media. You aren't selling. You are simply making your audience aware of what you have to offer in a way that is real and relatable.

By utilizing social media in this way, you will leave people better than you found them, which is the ultimate goal.

MASTER THE ART OF "JUST ENOUGH"

For those who are new to using social media for business, it can be intimidating. Are you over sharing? Are you under sharing? Or are you sharing "just enough?"

Don't worry about that right now. First let's talk about *what* you should share and the rest will mostly take care of itself. It's about mastering the art of *edutainment,* which is the combination of education and entertainment. In fact, those two words are the key—not advertising or promoting or anything else directly related to your agency.

Edutainment is the ideal approach to take on your personal page because it's the most effective, and also because it is against Facebook's policy to directly promote a business on your personal page. They have been known to shut down profiles for excessive promotion of a brand or company. Facebook requires that business promotions and direct advertising be restricted to business pages. That's fine with us because no one likes to be sold.

If you've ever picked up an issue of *US Weekly* magazine, you might have seen their regularly featured section called, "Stars: They're Just Like Us!" It's two pages of our favorite movie stars and musicians getting groceries, pumping gas, or dropping their ice cream (i.e., something relatable).

We love seeing this stuff! We love seeing them holding their kids' hands on the way home from school.

These are the kinds of real, relatable things we need to share as well.

You may sell insurance, but you are also a regular person with a life, a family, and goals that have nothing to do with what you do for a living. Open the curtains and let them in a little. Share the video of your daughter's piano recital. True fans and followers will love it.

You are just like them. Let them see that.

Your personal values and priorities should be a part of your overall mission. Social media blends both worlds together beautifully. Your life becomes a window—and it's amazing and humbling to let others take a look inside.

Important side note: It can't all be soccer games and date nights. Around 20 percent of your feed needs to be about business matters. Here's a great example of a live video intro that is a little bit of both:

> "To all you other 'mompreneurs' out there hustling to take care of the kids *and* working your butt off to grow your business, here's a 'mom hack' for making super quick, super healthy lunches for school…"

This video topic has nothing to do with growing a business. Yet it speaks to the fact that you too are a businessperson. You aren't selling anyone anything, but guess what? It's still a form of marketing!

As an insurance agent, you can do the same thing—educate, offer valuable advice, and let followers know you are a professional, all without directly selling. Here is an example of another live video opener:

"In my business I get asked the same question over and over: 'Is life insurance really important?' Is it? I mean, really? In our daily lives? It doesn't affect the way we get dressed in the morning. Life insurance doesn't make food taste better. But what about the 'what if's?' Are you prepared for the moments in life that no one expects? Like what if… [insert real stories from your customers' experiences]."

Post the video with a title that garners some attention or makes people curious (such as "C'mon, do we *really* need life insurance?") and you can accomplish a lot. It doesn't look anything like "normal" business promotion—and that's why it works.

We mentioned live videos a few times now. Is that all you should be putting out there? Of course not! Variety is the spice of life. Writing posts, uploading photos, and sharing other posts and interesting articles (known as curating content) are also important.

That said, there is something important you should know:

Live video is taking over, and yet right now, only a small percent of Facebook's two billion members are utilizing live video to reach their audience. That is insane!

This is your chance to be on the uptick of the live video trend. You'll stand out just by being one of the few who are doing it. If you are brave enough to do live videos (and it does get much easier after a few times), you will be at the top of every single friend's feed because—and this is really important—Facebook's algorithm prioritizes videos over other types of posts.

With time and intention, you'll learn tricks like this and more. We have studied what cover photos are the most effective, how to use Instagram to your advantage, and which social media platforms to use for certain demographics. These kinds of things are constantly changing, but since we recognize the importance of a social media presence in our business, we stay on top of them. If you want to stay relevant, you should, too.

HOW TO GROW YOUR FAN BASE

Whether you are a selfie-posting pro or new to social media, next we'll cover the basics of promoting your agency and yourself online in a productive, fun, and noninvasive way.

Facebook business pages have their place. However, those pages are primarily there to make Facebook money. Engagement on business pages often comes at a cost. If you have the extra funds to put into promoting your business, then go for it. But this type of social media activity is not what we're discussing here.

Business pages are important for many reasons—for credibility, for reviews, and more—but personal pages are often the best way to get an audience knowing you and loving you.

By methodically posting on your personal page, expanding your friend list, seeking mutual connections, and offering giveaways and fun opportunities, over time you can organically bring people over to your business page and build a massive audience there.

But it has to start on your personal page.

You may be wondering, "Well, that sounds great. But as of right now, my friend list consists of family, co-workers, and friends from high school."

Don't worry. We've all been there. Getting your video liked by your aunt and your mom is great, but that won't build any credibility for you. So, what do you do?

As we like to say, "your audience is your audience." You don't have to wait until you build some mythical perfect list of followers. Start with what you have. With the right posts and the right activity, you *will* eventually reach the people you are trying to reach.

As you embark on this new journey of social media expansion, take a good hard look at your cover photo and your bio. Is your profile picture a beach shot of you and your spouse in your swimsuits? These things matter. Consumers often buy based on first impressions. That means you have to look like a person *you* would do business with.

Go through your old pictures and delete ones that might hurt your credibility. Make sure you're an asset online, because people don't do business with people who won't make their lives better in some way. Always leave them better off.

HOW MUCH TIME TO SPEND ONLINE

This next topic is a tough one. Anyone who spends any time on Facebook knows it's easy to get dragged into the endless abyss of the "feed" and waste precious minutes, or even hours. So, we'll try to make this as straightforward as possible:

You should be posting at least one thing every day (three posts at a maximum), preferably in the morning, and then interact with that post and the responses briefly in scheduled moments throughout the day.

Plan times to check back in on your post to like comments and comment back. The more people you interact with throughout the day, the longer that post will stay at the top of the feed. You can even like and comment on your own post to bring it back to the top.

Each time you check in should take no more than a few minutes. Set a timer if you have to so you don't get sucked into the social media vacuum. Avoid the temptation to keep scrolling at all costs, because all that does is give you a front row seat to watching other people's dreams come true.

Instead, use your valuable time to pursue your own dreams.

Be intensely protective of your time!

It is also important to interact with other people's posts. It can't just be about you; in fact, it shouldn't be. We believe in reciprocity, which means that what you give comes back to you. Just make sure that when you click the like button, you really do like that person, because he or she will then start to show up in your feed more often.

We've found that people who are always doing videos get *really* annoying *really* quickly. One or two live videos a week is sufficient. Other than that, mix it up—from humor or a family story to a business hack or an inspirational quote.

If something amazing or funny happens to you, post about it!

Play around with the timing to find times of greatest engagement. It's not an exact science and can vary based on your audience. After work seems to be a great time to post. People are home and ready to unwind and are scrolling through their feeds looking to be entertained or amused. Live videos are also recommended in the evening because most people can't stop in the middle of the workday to watch a video.

Whatever activity level you choose, be consistent. Consistency will increase your following and your reach.

HOW TO ADD FRIENDS AND INFLUENCE PEOPLE

Organic growth is *slow*. However, you can accelerate the growth scale a little in ways that do not involve paid marketing or advertising:

1. Make it Public

First and foremost, you have to make your profile public. Nobody can find you if you're hidden. Some people think, "But what about safety and privacy?" Our answer is if there are certain things you don't want to share with the world, you can make those particular posts private or just for friends.

2. Join Groups

Find private Facebook groups with like-minded people. These groups do not have to be insurance based. Think about groups like entrepreneurs, working moms and dads, or other groups that will enable you to associate with users who might share your posts and have influencers following their posts. This can greatly expand your reach.

3. Take Suggestions Seriously

Facebook is always offering their suggestions for possible friends based on users having similar interests, friends in common, and more. Among these suggestions you'll likely find some folks in similar fields or living in your community.

4. Work New Contacts Every Week

We recommend actively working around *ten* new contacts a week that you find through suggestions and other groups. Keep this process simple. The most important thing is to interact with *their* posts and their activity. Make it about them—not you.

After a few days of interaction, send a private message, or even better, a voice message (Facebook has this feature) and say something like:

"Hey Jen, my name's Danelle. You came across my Facebook feed as a suggested friend. Your vacation post from a few days ago looked amazing! So jealous. We've visited close to where you stayed in the Bahamas. Anyway, you look like my kind of people. I'm in insurance, but I'm just connecting with like-minded folks in the area, and I'd love to get to know you a little better."

If they respond or add you, great! You've got a new connection to start getting to know, influencing, and helping. Check out your mutual connections. See what groups they interact with most. If they ignore your request and your message, move on and delete that request. You can have 25 requests out at a time. So as people accept or ignore you, add more.

If you want to grow your online platform, you have to treat it like a business. Some people "play around" with social media. If you play with it and don't use it consistently, don't expect big returns. However, if you take it seriously, it can deliver serious results. You can't expect a business to grow without putting in some work.

For us, a robust online presence is an integral part of our multi-million-dollar businesses, so we treat it as such.

BE YOU OR DON'T BOTHER

We've noticed a lot of people work hard to portray a certain online persona. We just have to ask:

Why work so hard to be someone you are not?

What about when people meet you in person? Who are you then? People want to know the real you. Just be the normal you both online and offline, whoever that is.

When people ask us how they should present themselves online, we tell them, "How did you make friends in elementary school?"

The answer is you asked questions and got to know your peers. You interacted. This is how it works no matter how old you are, and no matter whether you're on a playground or a laptop.

Just be a friend online and share your life.

People will share their trust and friendship in return.

Once you start doing this, you can use these real connections to build your business following. Here's a great example of this in action:

When someone reaches out to ask you a business-related question, let them know that if they go to your business page and like it, you'll post a live video every Friday night answering all the questions you got asked that week. That Friday night live video can be a fun and lively discussion with your viewers on topics related to your business—and they'll listen and respect you because you've been real with them and established yourself as a Trusted Advisor.

Become someone who solves people's problems better and more creatively than anyone else.

Be consistently online, let them get to know you, and you won't have to have so many of those "meet and greet" coffee appointments. Your new customers will already know you, and you both get to save some valuable time!

THE GREAT EQUALIZER

Social media is the great equalizer in business. Your agency, the mom and pop store down the street, the local farmer's market, and Fortune 500 corporations all have exactly the same opportunity to expand their reach and touch people's lives.

Social media can also be really kind or really tough on you. If you have killer customer service, it will be your best friend. If you mess up, people really like to share those negative experiences.

That's okay with us! It holds us accountable and keeps us on our toes. We make it our goal to take negative feedback (which is rare when you operate as a Trusted Advisor) and use it to make us better business builders, better agents, and better salespeople.

Old marketing is knocking on doors and using benches, billboards, and yellow pages ads. Today, social media is your billboard. Social media is your Sunday newspaper ad—and it's out there doing its job 24/7. All you must do is show up consistently to talk, share, train, and engage in edutainment. It really is the easiest place to grow your business.

It doesn't mean you forget the phones or any other part of our world. We still have to do our jobs. Social media is simply the perfect addition to what you are already doing.

Social media isn't going anywhere. In fact, its seismic growth indicates it will only become more influential. If you want to stay relevant, you've absolutely, positively got to take the conversation online.

Get consistent by posting at least once a day and start getting used to doing live videos (or pre-recorded if you're not ready). Just know that live video will get you more views.

You educate, and as you do, you build trust and stay top of mind.

Odds are many of your viewers won't even be in the market for insurance at the time. But by staying on their radar, when they *are* in the market, your name will surface.

You can be their instant choice for a Trusted Advisor simply by being a person that people are already used to seeing and hearing.

You *can* connect without selling.

And you can sell—simply by connecting.

Focus on Specialization

You may have inspirational meetings, killer contests, a world-class operations manual, and a well-defined sales path. But without the proper specialization, none of those things will ever do you any good.

Specialization, or segmentation, means putting the right butts in the right seats. When you put employees in their wheelhouse—into roles where they are most skilled—success is inevitable.

Everyone wore every hat during the first few years in our agencies. This worked just enough for us to stay in business, but it was not a recipe for success.

It didn't take long to recognize that people have specific talents and traits. Some are gifted at selling, some at taking care of clients, and some at doing paperwork and being organized. Our employees are now separated into three different departments: sales, the customer experience, and administration.

True salespeople need to be placed exclusively in that role. Those who excel at taking care of clients need a role where they can provide great customer experiences. Employees with strong organizational and paperwork skills should be given administrative roles that help the office run more efficiently.

Segment your office, and your business can change overnight. Each person will live up to their full potential because they will be doing something that fits their unique skill set.

People don't want to be forced to sell when they can't sell. People don't want to take care of clients when they don't have the patience to deal with the daily needs of existing clients. Those who are disorganized will never flourish in a more clerical role.

Don't shove square pegs into round holes. Have a process in place to make sure your people are doing what they do best, and you'll be on your way to a smooth-running agency.

CLEARLY DEFINE RESPONSIBILITIES

After placing everyone in their wheelhouse, the next step is to clearly define all responsibilities. Write a crystal-clear job description for every role so there are no gray areas.

We can't tell you how many times we've talked to other agency owners and their employees and discovered a massive disconnect. Here is what that usually sounds like:

The owner says, "My employees never do what I want them to do."

Their employees say, "We didn't even know our boss wanted us to do that; we had no idea that was part of our jobs."

We'll then ask the agency owner, "When did you tell them to do that? And where did you write that duty down?"

The answer should never be, "Well, they should just know."

If your staff doesn't know what their jobs really entail, it's not their fault. Never assume people "should just know" what they should being doing.

You have to spell it out for them.

When new employees start working for you, they should have clearly defined job descriptions that you have gone over with them, line by line. Everything must be laid out, so they know what they will be accountable for achieving.

For example, salespeople in our agencies understand they're expected to write a certain amount of business every month. If they meet that benchmark, they earn extra money. If they fail to hit their numbers for a consecutive number of months, they are terminated. This expectation is made clear from the beginning during training; it is written in our operations manual; it's also in their individual job descriptions.

We understand you have relationships with your team that transcend tasks and numbers. You spend a lot of time with them, and they're more than just employees. This doesn't negate the fact that expectations must be in place in order for the agency to succeed.

You will get what you expect in life, and too often we accept a lot less than we expect. Be careful about what you tell and do not tell your employees, and remember:

If you tell them nothing, then that is exactly what they'll do. Nothing. They will do just enough to pay their bills and not get fired until a better job comes along.

The more specific you are with the process, the better the results will be. When your team comes in every morning, make sure they know exactly what it is they are going to do that day. Some things obviously surface as the day progresses, but they should have no doubts as to what's expected of them.

You also have to know what's working and what's not. We're constantly refining and improving processes and asking for feedback from our teams.

Don't operate a "fly by the seat of your pants" agency. Carefully and intentionally define the process for your staff and inspect what you expect—and you will achieve the results you want.

DO YOUR JOB, DELEGATE THE REST

Earlier, we have mentioned that *duplication* is made possible through *delegation*—but in order to delegate correctly, you must also practice specialization.

Instead of running a generalist model where everyone does everything, but nobody is really amazing at any one thing, you can amplify your results by allowing people to specialize and therefore hone their unique skills.

The last thing you want is for any of your employees to consider themselves to be a "jack of all trades, master of none." This applies to you, too.

If you value your time at $500 an hour, or even just $50 an hour, why would you personally do any job that you could pay someone else $10, $15, or $20 an hour to do? That doesn't make sense.

If you value your time at more than $1,000 an hour, why would you take time out of your schedule to do something you could pay someone else $50 or even $100 an hour to do?

You only have so many hours in a day, and we only have so much time in our lives. Go do the tasks that only you can do, and delegate the hourly tasks to others.

SPECIALIZED BABY STEPS

Once you define which role works best for each employee, we recommend you start each employee off in an entry-level position, no matter their level of experience.

Here is a timeline of how that would look for a new hire in the *sales department*:

A new hire starts out as a *sales trainee* working under a sales manager's direction. After 90 days, he has an opportunity to become a licensed agent.

After a year of succeeding in the role of *licensed agent*, he has an opportunity to lead others as a *sales manager*. He would then be responsible for recruiting and training one or more sales trainees under him while receiving a small commission on all the agents he recruited and trained during that time.

Override commission is paid on a tier basis, which gives the sales manager incentive to find success right out of the gate, as it's a declining commission override. In other words, he makes the most in the first 90 days, and it tiers down every 90 days for one year, until it becomes a flat number forever, unless the trainee becomes a sales manager.

After hiring and training three agents as the sales manager, this individual could be placed in another location as an *operations manager*. Finally, at the very top, he could either purchase that location at a predetermined price or be considered for another role that includes overseeing multiple locations.

A new hire in the *service department* would be presented with a similar path:

He starts out as a *customer service trainee* while in training under a service rep. As a trainee, he can become a *licensed customer service representative*, a position in which he handles client reviews and other complex customer issues.

After succeeding in this role, he can move on to the *office manager* role for an individual location. Next, he can become the *area office manager* for all locations, overseeing each agency's office manager and customer service reps.

Using this stair-step approach to advancement provides your employees with real, tangible career goals that incentivize them to grow more and more skilled in their specialized areas.

Your team wants to be inspired and work toward a common goal that tells them exactly what success looks like in your organization. Give them the path to success by placing them in roles that fit their unique skill sets, objectives, and tastes.

Place people in their wheelhouse and you will set the revenue train in motion.

Emphasize Ownership and Accountability

In the most successful agencies, everybody has their own unique job description. Everybody understands what they need to do. But does that always mean it will get done? Probably not.

After a while, without the right checks and balances in place—and without continually inspecting what you expect—people will eventually slack off in certain areas.

It doesn't mean they're lazy. It just means they're human.

Everyone needs a reminder from time to time, which is why we have ownership meetings.

WHAT ARE OWNERSHIP MEETINGS?

Our futures hang on the success of our agencies. It's a feeling that either motivates agency owners to succeed or causes them such stress that they operate with a crippling fear of failure.

We certainly don't want our employees to feel the same level of pressure that we feel, but we do want them to *own* their position. We want it to be theirs—and that's what the ownership meetings are all about.

Whenever your employees see an opportunity to make an improvement or tweak something, you ideally want them to bring it to your attention. If their advice makes sense, you can run with it.

This way, you all get better together.

When you give your team some autonomy, they feel like they're part of the process. They feel like they are on a mission *with* you, rather than just working *for* you.

Each month, we meet with every employee one-on-one for a 20- to 30-minute ownership meeting. Here is a typical ownership meeting agenda:

1. Review the Previous Month.

The first few minutes of the meeting are spent reviewing the previous month. For a salesperson, we review every item they wrote, how much premium they wrote, and how many quotes they did. Were they on time each morning? How many hours did they log? We briefly discuss every aspect of their performance for the past 30 days.

2. Inspect What You Expect.

We take this opportunity to inspect what we expect. For example, let's say for a salesperson, the minimum requirement is to write 40 items and at least $15,000 in production per month. Additionally, they cannot be late to work more than twice. If they fail to meet an expectation, they get a warning. If they get three warnings, they are terminated.

3. Ask Them How They Did.

As agency owners, we can be quick to point out the negatives. They could have done many things correctly and wrote a ton of business, but they were also late several mornings. The natural tendency is to latch onto that and glide over the accomplishments.

Next time, instead of highlighting their mistakes, ask a simple question:

"Is there any area where you feel you could have done better?"

After you ask this question, remain quiet, and allow them to speak freely. We have found that most employees are much harder on themselves than we would ever be on them.

Pushing back against criticism is human nature. But when people correct *themselves*, it clicks, and it often sounds like this: "I did this part of my job well, but I shouldn't have been late so many times. I understand that is not what I should have done. It won't happen again."

This makes your job so much easier! All you have to say is, "You're right. You've done all these other things very well, and next month I expect the same. Just clean up that one area; but overall, great job!"

It's your job to point out the good—and then use the key question to let *them* point out where they need to improve.

4. Set Next Month's Goals.

At the end of the review, we discuss goals for the coming month. We ask staff to set three business goals and one personal goal.

The personal goal is just as essential as the business goals because these are not just your employees—they are your work family. It's critical to understand what is important to them.

Whether they want to have regular date nights with their partner, get to the gym in the mornings, read two books a week, or spend more time with their children, you now know their priorities. With that knowledge, you can better invest in them and in their future with your agency.

When you treat your employees like family by making an effort to understand what is really important to them, it will come back to you tenfold.

‖‖‖

Ownership meetings can revolutionize your agency.

They are brief, powerful, and informative. It is critical that they take place consistently, so that you and your employees can clearly nail down what is expected from month to month.

People will never be confused about what you expect, because you communicate it so clearly and so often! No one will ever be surprised when you have to terminate an employee because they all know what is expected in each role.

Zig Ziglar said, "Repetition is the mother of learning, the father of action, which makes it the architect of accomplishment." If you want your team to be better, if you want to get the most out of them, if you want them to work to their fullest potential and produce at high levels, then you must hold them accountable for doing the right actions over and over again. While doing this, you must also help them take ownership of their role.

Be consistent and keep your expectations clear and simple, and accelerated growth will follow.

THE BIG H.E.R.O. TAKE-AWAY

Everyone gets into the insurance business for unique reasons. Maybe you want to have more control over your time and be able to do the things you want to do, when you want to do them.

It may not seem like your time and your life are your own right now. You're scratching your head and reflecting that you never thought you'd have to work this hard at anything.

Running a successful business is hard—just ask all the people who fail (and there are a lot).

We have all failed, too, but the difference is we never gave up.

We pushed past the difficult years when it seemed like there wasn't enough time or capital to continue. We pushed past the doubt and the fear because our why's were too big to ignore.

We also listened to the advice of our mentors and those who had already achieved what we wanted. We learned from them and stopped trying to reinvent the wheel.

Today, we are in a position where we can do what we want to do, whenever we want to do it. We have tremendous freedom. And to us, that's the true definition of success.

Do you want to build a business that runs without you? Do you want to have agencies in multiple states? Do you want to stay close to home so you can spend more time with your family?

Whatever your why, the only way to get there is to set up systems that enable you to automate your operations.

You never want to miss a single one of your kids' games? That can be your reality. You want to travel the world? That can be your reality. That's the beautiful thing about the profession you've chosen—the sky really is the limit.

If you want to take your agency to another level, and if you want to have work-life balance, having well-defined operations within your agency is key. This includes a solid staffing structure where things are delegated and duplicated; it also includes specialization, where all employees know their roles and what is expected of them.

While it's going to take a lot of time, investment, and hard work, we assure you it will be well worth it.

At the end of the day, this is still just work. Outside your agency, you have a whole other life and people you love. Don't make your business your life.

No one has ever been lying on his or her deathbed wishing to have worked more hours. It's much likelier we'll reach our golden years wishing we'd spent more time with our family.

When you have a great system, it will prevent you from becoming a prisoner of your agency. You can spend more time doing things you love, not be filled with fear that your business is going to fail, because you've set it up to operate the same whether you're there or not.

Build a business that creates freedom.

Build a business that serves and benefits you, but also serves your employees and your clients.

There are numerous systems and processes to instill in your agency. You need a sales process, annual review process, claims follow-up process, marketing process, and training process. You must also define when and how to prospect, establish clear communication, foster a sense of ownership in your employees, and delegate.

That's a lot to consider, but the great news is you are already on the right track—so continue becoming a student of your craft, and you will create one of the best agencies in this industry.

It's as hard as people think it will be, because even though there are plenty of good agents and agencies, what takes the most work, as author Jim Collins says, is going from *good* to *great*.

The difference between good and great rests in your ability to learn and grow. You can begin by applying the principles in this book.

We'd say good luck to you, but luck in our business only comes to those who work to receive it. So instead, we'll say: Get to work.

Become a
Trusted Advisor

I t was the best of times for one salesperson.

It was the worst of times for another.

Paul is in insurance sales, and he believes every day in his career is exciting and filled with opportunities to help others.

Joe is also in insurance sales, but to him, every day is exhausting and filled with the monotonous tasks of a job he took when he was out of options.

Paul wakes up at 5:00 A.M. "Today is going to be a great day," he says, as he looks around his family's dream house. He is thankful he can afford the best private school for his kids and the best vacations every year for his family. He puts on his workout clothes and heads out the door for a morning run while listening to this week's motivational book on his earbuds.

Joe's alarm goes off at 6:30 A.M. but he hits the snooze until almost 7:00 A.M., moaning and groaning with each annoying buzz. As he wipes the sleep from his eyes, he mutters, "Why can't it be Friday already?" He looks around his house, which needs every kind of repair, and thinks with a loud sigh, "Why can't I ever catch a break?" He stumbles into his closet and attempts to find a shirt that isn't stained and will still fit over a belly that has been overloaded with too many fast-food meals.

Paul returns home exhilarated by his run. He showers and dresses in a well-tailored suit and polished shoes. He sips coffee at the kitchen table and spends a few minutes with the most important people in his life, his lovely wife and their great kids. He's grateful his job allows him the freedom to go on several vacations a year and take plenty of long weekends. He blends a green power smoothie for the road, kisses his family goodbye, and is on the road by 6:15 A.M.

Joe trips over a pile of toys at the bottom of the stairs and grumbles loud enough for everyone to hear, "Why can't they put their stuff away!" The family is getting ready for school, and as he watches his kids, he wishes he had more time and especially more energy to spend with them, but his job is "just too exhausting." He grabs a bagel with his coffee and is out the door by 7:30 A.M. "The traffic better not be as bad as usual today," he says under his breath as his aging sedan struggles to start. He doesn't want to be late again. He can't bear another lecture from the boss.

Paul arrives at the office at 6:45 A.M. He likes to get to the office first. He uses the quiet time to go over his schedule for the day, look at his goals, and do some continuing education. As an added bonus, he loves missing rush hour traffic and the stress that goes along with it.

Joe's hopes about traffic are dashed as he sees a minor traffic accident has turned the interstate into a parking lot. "Great," he thinks, "I really can't catch a break. And I bet none of these idiots have their coverage through us." He's the last to arrive at the office. It's 8:14 A.M. He tries to slither into the morning meeting unnoticed.

Paul sees on his calendar that he has a meeting scheduled with one of his long-time clients, Amy Jordan, to discuss her policies up for renewal. He loves reconnecting with customers and finding out how their jobs are going, how their kids are doing, and how he can help them. "Helping people" is not some meaningless phrase to him. He loves doing business with people who listen to him and understand him and his unique situation, so why wouldn't his customers want to be treated the same way? It's just good business.

Joe knows his micromanaging sales manager expects him to make at least 100 calls that day, but he is just not ready for all of the "not interested" responses he will hear. As he picks up the phone to start smiling and dialing, he wonders where it all went wrong. How did he end up here, telephoning strangers all day, as a glorified telemarketer?

As Paul begins his morning phone time, he breaks down his goals for the day. He likes to "eat the elephant" one bite at a time, and it also reminds him to slow down and connect with everyone. Treating people like numbers has never helped his bottom line. He realized a long time ago that the key is to treat everyone according to the old-fashioned Golden Rule. He also knows most people are underinsured—and that puts them and their families at risk. He's made it his mission to teach as many people as he can what being "protected" looks like.

Joe leaves dry voicemail after voicemail as he thinks, "Why do we bother cold calling anymore? No one answers their phones." The minutes creep by in slow motion, as he hopes and prays *someone* will agree to meet with him so he can talk about how his products are better and cheaper. Lunch hour arrives in the nick of time—he can't take one more rude prospect. "No one gets it," he thinks. "Well, whatever happens to them, they deserve it."

Paul's customer, Amy, comes in just after lunch, and Paul is happy to see his client and friend again. Amy has been doing business with their agency for four years, and over the course of their relationship, she has moved all of her policies over to Paul. She also referred her parents and in-laws, two of her closest friends, and a number of her co-workers. As they reconnect, she fills him in on her husband's new job and the twins' new school. She needs to change her coverage and has some questions, and Paul is ready with educated responses. He also has some follow-up questions for her to ensure that she has the same level of protection Paul would recommend to members of his own family.

After lunch, Joe sets a few appointments (even a broken clock is correct twice a day, right?). He was in the right place at the right time when some prospects shopping around for some new policies called the office. Without asking any other questions or even knowing whether they are existing customers, Joe assures them he can give them an absolutely unbeatable price, hangs up the phone, and emails quotes to them right away. Satisfied with himself as he presses send, he thinks, "I'll finally have some good news for my boss."

Paul's last call of the day comes in at 4:45 P.M. One of his customers, Mr. Howard, was injured in an accident a few days earlier, and bills are already pouring in. Paul takes his time and explains once again how the claims process works and goes over Mrs. Howard's coverage until he fully understands. By the end of the conversation, Mr. Howard can't stop thanking Paul for helping him and doing all of the heavy lifting, so Mr. Howard can focus on his recovery.

At 4:45 P.M., Joe starts going through the motions of working, when in reality, he's already logged off his computer and is ready to run out the door and be in his car by 5:01 P.M. As his foot hits the pavement on the way out, he's wondering when enough will be enough and he finally finds a "more respectable job" with a nice, comfortable base salary.

As Paul wraps up the call with Mr. Howard around 5:30 P.M., he gets excited about seeing his family that evening. "Maybe we can go out for dinner and talk about our upcoming Disney trip," Paul thinks. He had some great conversations today. Some of them led to appointments; a few led to some new business; all of them grew his confidence and his reputation as a Trusted Advisor. He is so thankful to have found a career that allows him to help people all day long and gives him the opportunity to make more money than he ever thought he could make, as well as the freedom to spend time doing what he loves.

‖‖‖‖

So, what is Joe's major problem? Besides his overall pessimistic attitude and lack of personal drive, he seems to have committed the same mistake as the majority of other agents and the general public:

He has *commoditized* insurance.

When you make it all about the number of policies you can sell, it prevents you from seeing past the commission and looking at the individual.

Agents also tend to think "with their own pockets." When they do, it becomes next to impossible for them to recommend any coverage that they themselves can't or won't consider. It is this kind of small thinking that defers dreams, causes dissatisfaction, and perpetuates harmful stereotypes of salespeople.

Think these stories are make-believe? At some point in our careers, we (and the people who work alongside us) have resembled aspects of both men.

"Average Joe" is the standard in our industry; he represents what most agents think their jobs will be like and how they tend to think—he also represents what most customers expect from an insurance agent.

How can we transform our agencies into offices filled with Aspirational Pauls and rid ourselves of the Average Joes? It's really simple:

Stop selling and start helping.

If you've been in this business for more than a week, you already know more about insurance than 99 percent of the population. It then becomes your job not just to take an order and fill the needs customers *think* they have—it's your job to demonstrate your experience and knowledge in a way that accomplishes two things:

- Enable customers to feel confident in what you are saying.
- Enable customers to see how confident *you* are in what you are saying.

If you have ever done business with a salesperson who takes the time to find out about you and your unique situation, didn't you walk out of that encounter feeling amazing? Someone took *their* time to hear *you*! Miracles still happen!

The cold, hard truth is that no one does that anymore. Anywhere. No one takes the time to ask a few questions and authentically listen.

People are not metrics.

People are not their policies.

This isn't about changing your priorities and transforming into some softer, warmer version of yourself. You can still be driven to sell more, and you can still aspire to be as wealthy as you want to be. In fact, it's in the pursuit of increasing your bottom line that caring and connecting become more important than ever!

The most successful professionals we know take their time. They value education, and they listen far more than they speak.

Don't overcomplicate this game; it really can be simple.

As this book draws to a close, let's talk about simple ways to help you and everyone in your agency earn the coveted and lucrative title of Trusted Advisor.

THE GREATEST JOB IN THE WORLD

If you can relate to Average Joe's plight in some way, we get it. We've all been there. Sales is the toughest job in the world. But it's tough for a good reason—no other career on earth offers you the potential for limitless income. When you were young, let's say someone had come to career day and said:

> "Okay, kids, you have two options: you can go to school and train for 10+ years after high school, work 80 hours a week, get two weeks of paid vacation and make $250,000 a year as a doctor. You could also go to college (or not) and work 50 to 60 hours a week for the first few years setting up systems to automate your business. After a while, you're making money in your sleep thanks to the power of renewals. You wake up a few years later and realize that you can go on vacation when you want, take off early on a Friday, and eventually make high six figures or even seven figures a year, literally just by talking to people every day."

Which one would you choose? That's right! You have the best job in the world. Don't ever let anyone tell you otherwise, and don't ever allow someone else's perception of your career affect how you do your job.

That can be easier said than done. When most people think of "insurance agent" a lot of words come to mind, and most of those words are not complimentary. The public views people in our profession as peddlers and order takers who are slimy, unprofessional, and potentially unethical.

Those of us who are serious about turning our jobs into lifelong, lucrative, and rewarding careers face an uphill battle. That is why we have devoted this final chapter to the most important truth you will ever hear in your business. Ready for it? Here it is:

You will never achieve the kind of success you really want until you foster and maintain a reputation for being a Trusted Advisor.

You've seen that phrase a lot in this book—and that's because it is the critical and indispensable foundation upon which we have built our businesses.

Let's review our definition of Trusted Advisor from Chapter 10.

Trusted Advisor [noun]:
An insurance expert and "people person" who values maintaining a relationship more than the outcome of any particular transaction.

Trusted Advisors promise two things:

1. We protect the assets our clients work so hard to attain.
2. We assist customers in accumulating the assets they'll need to retire comfortably.

That sounds nice, and we'd love to give you a simple trick for making it happen, but becoming a Trusted Advisor is not a decision you make and then it's done.

It's a process, and it doesn't happen overnight. In fact, the major drawback to becoming a Trusted Advisor is the amount of time it takes to earn this title.

When you take the road less traveled, it always takes longer. The front-end work is greater—conversations are longer, and the education is more intense and more ongoing.

But who wins the race in the end—the tortoise or the hare?

Trusted Advisors are the tortoises of the insurance industry. And we always win.

We take extra time and ask the right questions. We do things right the first time, because we never want any of our customers to be "the one."

The one who slips through the cracks.

The one who ends up suffering because we did not do our job properly.

The one who came into the office with coverage questions, but you were in such a big hurry that day that you didn't take the time to listen. So, you answer as quickly as you can and send him on his way. A few days later, he gets into an accident and after that, a major lawsuit. He calls you and asks, "Why didn't you tell me about umbrella policies? I could have been protected from all of this!"

You can create the kind of agency that leaves everyone better off. It just takes the right mindset and actions, day in and day out. In the final section, we will define the mindsets and actions of a Trusted Advisor so that you and everyone in your agency earn this title in the eyes of your customers and the community.

HOW TO BECOME A TRUSTED ADVISOR

When we think of a typical salesperson, one word comes to mind more than any other: *transactional.*

The word "transactional" itself is boring. It's checking a box. It's placing a tick mark on the board. It's a numbers game.

It's the worst.

Sadly, that is how the majority of salespeople approach their jobs. It's an approach devoid of heart that will lead to failure, or at best, mediocrity.

What is the alternative? You can go from being transactional to *relational.*

The phrase "relationship building" is overused. As a result, it's lost a lot of its impact. This is unfortunate for salespeople, since relationships are the key to success in our industry.

If you want to close more business, you could increase your daily call quota from 100 to 200 calls a day, *or* you could change your approach to the calls you are already making.

You could connect to people in a way that naturally leads to a greater closing percentage, increased retention, and a fuller book of business.

This means you will probably end up making even fewer calls because your calls will last longer, but the end result will be significantly improved.

Which one sounds more appealing?

We agree.

If you are ready to change your approach and make more out of every connection, here are eight of the most important actions to start implementing in your office.

Expect these actions from everyone—and always follow through by inspecting what you expect.

1. Be Authentic.

When you walk onto a car lot, you can sense the desperation. The salespeople descend upon you like moths to a flame. It's annoying, and at no point during the process do you think, "This salesperson just wants what's best for me."

Most prospects looking for insurance products feel the same way about insurance salespeople.

People can sense insincerity a mile away, so one of the easiest ways to start overcoming this stereotype is to never say something unless you actually mean it. Become known for your integrity. Clichéd sound bites and slogans do not win over lifelong customers. Lifelong customers will come when you are authentic and straightforward with them.

2. Be a Good Listener.

When managing sales teams, we find that the top salespeople are driven by curiosity. Questions like, "So what do you do for a living?" are fine, but top performing agents love to dig in and find out even more. Rather than find out the basics (job, married, kids) and move on, tee up the conversation with something like, "Walk me through a typical day for you." Then sit back and listen as you imagine what their day really looks and feels like.

Listen—because information is power. Most people don't pay attention, but Trusted Advisors:

- Empathize, summarize, and clarify until they are confident they fully understand the unique situation of each customer.
- Minimize distractions such as cell phones when they are with customers.
- Make eye contact. You cannot listen without eye contact.

- Smile. All day long. Both in person and on the phone. Prospects can *hear* a smile over the phone.
- Control body movements, because body language says more than our words.

It's not that hard to stand out. Ask people about their day or their last vacation, and then shut up and pay attention! Ask follow-up questions to demonstrate that you are actually listening.

When you show a heightened level of interest, clients will be more open with you. What's even better, you will be able to identify more opportunities through deeper discussions.

Empower your entire staff to be inquisitive and curious. Every call from a client is an opportunity to deepen the relationship and find new ways to help that client get the protection he or she needs.

3. Be Honest.

Honesty is always the best policy. Unfortunately, salespeople are not known for their honesty. Comedians usually lump us in with politicians.

It's time to challenge some stereotypes. If you say you want to help others but instead are focused on what you want to get out of the relationship, this becomes obvious to clients.

If you are serious about building real relationships, the focus must be on what is best for them—and sometimes that means telling them that your products won't meet their specific needs at this time. As much as we'd like to provide the best solutions for absolutely everyone, this is just not realistic. Admitting this truth can actually strengthen your reputation as a Trusted Advisor.

4. Be Dependable.

Trusted Advisors keep their promises, without exception. If you are continually failing to do what you said you would, your customers will lose respect for you and their faith in your ability to deliver on your promises. If you tell a client you will follow up with her by a certain date, do it. If you tell someone you will find the answer to an important question, find it.

If you want to be trusted, you must also be dependable. When clients know you keep your promises and deliver on time, they will relax, safe in the knowledge that you will look after them.

5. Be an Expert.

Some of the professionals we more naturally trust are doctors, lawyers, and professors. What do these professions have in common? It took a lot of schooling and studying to earn those titles. It would seem, then, that *education* has a lot to do with the level of trust someone is willing to place in another person.

Trusted Advisors focus on continual education. Clients are more likely to listen to your recommendations when they regard you as a credible, authoritative expert on the matter at hand.

Does this mean you need to go back to school? No. In our business, there are countless ways to keep learning without formal schooling. Learn the right language that helps a client assess your credibility, and display a high level of confidence when talking about a particular subject. Continually enriching your professional skills and knowledge is a key part of building credibility with clients.

You are the second most important professional in people's lives. It's a doctor's job to keep us alive and well, and it's our job to protect that life and everything in it. What an incredible responsibility. Once you truly grasp the full weight of it, you can begin to view your job in the same way doctors do.

When you go into a doctor's office, she controls the conversation by asking the right questions, obtaining information, and discovering what she needs to know to make sound recommendations. Can you imagine walking into a doctor's office and saying, "No tests for me today, doc. I just need that drug I saw on TV, and I'll be on my way."

That sounds crazy, and yet so-called professionals in our industry allow customers to do this to them all day long! Customers walk in, quote a price they saw on a commercial that featured a cuddly animal, and expect you to be a robotic order taker.

It's time to take control. Take the power back and lead the conversation in the way that only a trusted insurance expert can.

6. Be a Storyteller.

It's next to impossible to find a responsible adult who doesn't understand the logic behind why we need insurance. It just makes sense, and the majority of individuals know why they have to have it.

But understanding the logic behind something doesn't necessarily drive people to act. More than half of Americans die without a will, though nearly everyone agrees having one is important.

All those insurance commercials tell consumers how much money they can save by switching to this or that carrier. There are a lot of options out there, and in reality, what you have to offer is nothing special. However, there is one way to make your offerings stand out from the crowd.

You are what set your products apart, through your efforts to build emotional connections with clients on a personal and business level.

When you listen and learn about another human being's life, it enables you to understand and connect with his or her values and beliefs. Deeper conversations help build vital emotional connections and provide insight into what drives behavior.

People love stories—they love to tell them, and they definitely prefer to hear a good story over listening to boring facts and figures.

Connect through stories filled with vivid imagery. Brush up on your storytelling skills and watch what it does to strengthen your relationships and your business.

7. Be Unmistakably Passionate.

We all admire those people who can light up a room when they walk into it. No matter our own personality type, we are naturally drawn to people who are passionate and enthusiastic. Successful people often cite being around passionate people as a major factor in their own success—and this is absolutely true in your business.

You can have the greatest products in the world and offer the best service to your customers, but if you can't get excited about it, why should anyone else?

Passion and enthusiasm are contagious. It's nearly impossible not to smile or start laughing when someone around you is laughing uncontrollably. This doesn't mean you have to start telling jokes during your next meeting, but it does mean that smiles, positive body language, and enthusiasm matter. Your clients are much less likely to come back if you are dull, boring, and unenthusiastic. Life is too short to be bored by our insurance agents, so have a little fun, smile, and share some laughs.

8. Be Focused on the Long Term.

Outside the office, what is one thing that your strongest relationships have in common? More than likely, they are the ones you've had the longest.

Clients are not loyal to a salesperson who is only interested in getting an order, doesn't listen to them, and isn't interested in them as an individual. Those are traits of a *transactional* salesperson—and while this type of approach may produce some results in the short term, it is unlikely to lead to a profitable relationship in the long term.

Another big reason to think long term and focus on relationships is this: People tell other people about those rare salespeople who actually listen and care. Word of mouth recommendation is not something you can *buy*; it's an honor and a privilege you can only *earn*. It's also the most powerful and effective form of advertising, and it's far more likely to happen if you focus on building long-term relationships with your clients.

||||||

When you ask anyone what it takes to be a great salesperson, you will hear things like, *resilience, integrity, patience, listening skills, not pushy,* and *persistence*.

Want to know what these traits have in common? They can't be taught in a classroom. Sales can be an art and a science at times, but when you boil it down, sales is about human connection.

It is the people-to-people, face-to-face relationships that will make or break your career.

Prioritizing relationships is the most direct and intentional route we have found to grow our businesses in a way that achieves our long-term goal of sustained, consistent, and scalable success.

Becoming a Trusted Advisor is good for everyone—it's great for your customers because they finally get to be heard and get the protection they deserve. It's great for you because those customers will come back to you and bring their friends and family with them.

That's just how life works. Put good out there and it comes back to you. Trying to do it any other way is inefficient and a real waste of everyone's time.

Performing the actions of a Trusted Advisor, as Paul said in the beginning of the chapter, is "just good business." If you want to run a top agency, no other road will get you there. Start by displaying these actions yourself, and watch as your team imitates these behaviors and it spreads throughout the agency at every level.

In the same way that one negative attitude can poison the well, the right actions can spur the results you are really after and cultivate agency-wide success.

Our mentors taught us the simple truth that "people do not care how much you know until they know how much you care." A Trusted Advisor is someone who cares, who sees past stereotypes, and who understands that the person they are speaking with deserves to be heard.

If you have to tell customers, "I'm a Trusted Advisor," you aren't one.

Trusted Advisors prove their status through their actions.

No one on your team will achieve the title of Trusted Advisor until each person is living and breathing the desire to focus on relationships rather than transactions.

Earning this title takes time and can only happen one customer at a time. Focus on building relationships—one conversation at a time—and watch how far your business will go!

Ready for more? Visit us at AgencySalesAcademy.com for our schedule of upcoming events and to find out more about coaching opportunities for every stage of your business.

We are ready to help you become a Hero!

AGENCY SALES ACADEMY LIVE EVENTS

READY TO TRANSFORM YOUR AGENCY?

At ASA Live Events, you will learn from four top-producing agency owners and two business growth and customer service experts. You'll walk away with specific systems and processes that they use to ACCELERATE their agency GROWTH every single year.

Let Agency Sales Academy and our record-busting top producers show your agents exactly what they do each and every day to put up numbers ranging from 80 to 150 items a month—by themselves!

Come to the next event and bring your key staff members with you for a steep discount on their tuition. We look forward to seeing you and your team there!

To purchase tickets for our next live event, please visit:

AGENCYSALESACADEMY.COM/EVENT

AGENCY SALES ACADEMY COACHING

Want to Motivate Your Employees, Expand Your Book of Business, and Accelerate Your Growth?

That is what our Coaching Programs are designed to do! ASA Coaching will show agency owners and their team members how to thrive in ANY MARKET. Here are some of the benefits of joining ASA's Masters Level Program:

- **Access to All ASA Processes and Supporting Documents** that include: process and training manuals, our ten-step hiring process and our agency handbook.
- **Agency Owner Training** that includes: buying and selling agencies, maximizing agency revenue, hiring high performing staff, creating a winning environment, and building a successful scratch agency.
- **Staff Sales Training** that includes: sales process training, prospecting, closing strategies, asking for recommendations, advanced sales techniques, and building centers of influence through mortgage brokers and social media.
- **Staff Service Training** that includes: doing customer protection reviews, improving retention through exceptional service, creating raving fans, onboarding service staff, and setting appointments.
- **Weekly Video Conference Calls** with ASA founders on "hot topics" and open Q&As with special guests that include: interviews with the best agents across the country, high profile speakers, industry experts, and of course, the ASA co-founders and our strategic partners.
- **The ASA "Treasure Chest"** with more than 50 proven strategies to increase customer engagement and overall satisfaction.

For more information, please visit:

AGENCYSALESACADEMY.COM/COACHING